Art Nouveau

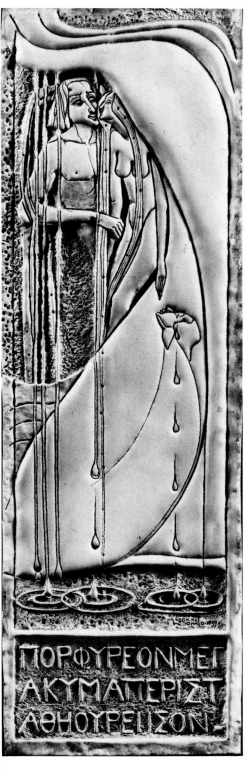

Art Nouveau

MARIA COSTANTINO

MAGNA
BOOKS

Published by Magna Books
Magna Road
Wigston
Leicester LE18 4ZH

Produced by
Bison Books Ltd
Kimbolton House
117A Fulham Road
London SW3 6RL

ISBN 1-85422-502-2

Printed in Spain

Reprinted 1994

PAGE 1: *A pair of decorative panels designed by the Macdonald sisters,
Frances and Margaret, in 1899.*

PAGE 2: *Detail of a painted panel by Margaret Macdonald Mackintosh
designed for Miss Cranston's Tea Rooms at 199 Sauchiehall Street,
Glasgow.*

Contents

The
Applied
Arts

Any distinction between the fine arts and the applied arts is really a matter of convenience as far as Art Nouveau is concerned; its practitioners abhorred any such categorization. Their aim was to break down those very barriers. For Art Nouveau designers, each art was of equal importance, and many designers excelled in several art forms in an effort to create the unified design that was their ideal. The silverware in the shape of flowers, for example, was the work of Prince Bogdan Karageorgevitch, an artist whose work could be found at the *Maison Moderne* who was also a writer and journalist. Many so called 'applied artists' such as Henri van de Velde gave up promising careers as painters to produce metalwork, tapestries and furniture. Van de Velde's first applied art work was for book illustrations and tapestries such as *La Verillée des Anges*, but his qualities as a designer are more evident in the smaller objects like the teasets he designed for Meissen Dresden or his silver samovars and candlesticks, where the lines are worked according to the function and structure of the object being decorated.

But the Art Nouveau designers did not confine themselves to precious materials such as silver: they also used brass, copper, pewter and iron, all materials that had previously been dismissed as largely utilitarian, suitable only for the 'baser' objects such as door handles, simple vessels and cooking utensils. Now designers showed that it was possible to use these 'base' materials to produce works of art, and that no object was too insignificant to be beautiful: finger plates, door knobs and lock plaques like those designed by Alexandre Charpentier in 1896 and commissioned by the firm of Fontaine, bear witness to the influence of Art Nouveau.

In England the outstanding contribution to the range of metalwork being produced was made by a range of pewterware by Liberty and Co of Regent Street. Arthur Lazenby Liberty had employed many of the leading designers of the day such as Voysey, Arthur Wilcox, Arthur Silver and Archibald Knox. Arthur Silver (1853-1896) opened his own studio in 1880 where he concentrated on producing a range of textiles for Liberty and Co in inexpensive materials, suitable for middle- and lower-class homes and pockets. Silver's son Rex (1879-1965) continued his father's work by designing a wide range of household objects and jewelry in silver. But a unique venture in metalwork on the part of Liberty was the silverware launched under the Celtic name *Cymric* (pronounced Kum-rick). Cymric silver

proved so popular that Liberty believed that a less expensive range of domestic ware in pewter, called *Tudric* but designed along the same lines, would be equally successful. *Tudric* pewter made its appear-

ABOVE: *This silver samovar was designed by Henri van de Velde in 1902.*

LEFT: *The firm of Georg Jensen of Copenhagen successfully adapted designs such as this 1922 silver vessel by Johan Rohde to suit machine methods of production.*

RIGHT: *Despite the widespread introduction of electric lighting at the end of the nineteenth century, designers still produced candelabras and candlesticks. In this piece by Henri van de Velde, the silver is worked into lines that resemble the molten wax of the candles.*

BELOW LEFT: *No detail escaped the eye of the Art Nouveau designers, nor was any object considered too prosaic to be beautiful. These door handles were designed for Dunglass Castle by Talwin Morris in 1898-99.*

BELOW RIGHT: *These spoons based on Celtic designs, possibly by Archibald Knox, come from the 'Cymric' range of silverware marketed by Liberty and Co. The center spoon was produced as a souvenir of the coronation of Edward VII.*

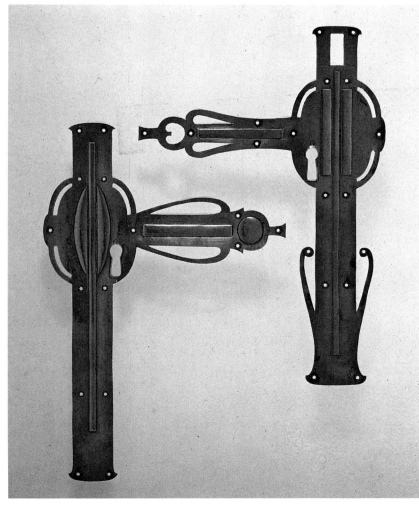

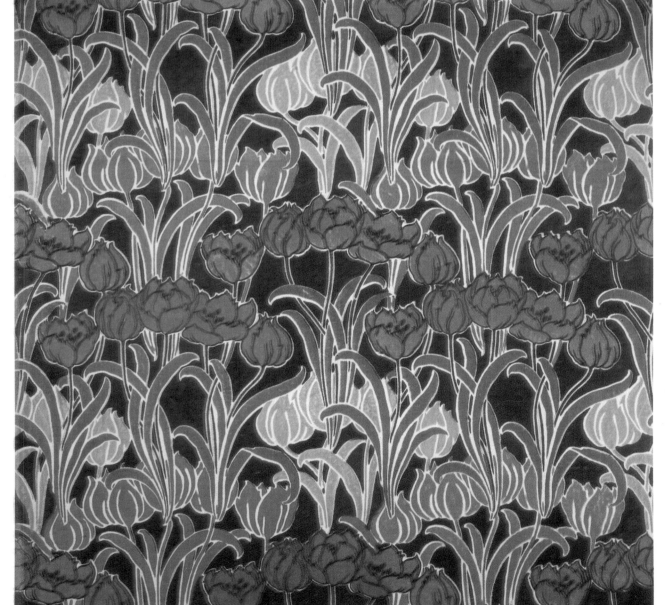

ABOVE: *This lizard door handle on a house in the Avenue Rapp, Paris, was designed by Lavirotte in 1901.*

LEFT: *Arthur Silver supplied Liberty and Co with a range of textile designs suitable for the growing number of middle-class homes of the 1890s.*

RIGHT: *These 'Tudric' pewter clocks designed by Archibald Knox c 1903-4 and made by Liberty and Co, filled the demand for less expensive items in the same style at the 'Cymric' silver. With both 'Tudric' and 'Cymric,' decorative enamels were often used.*

ance around 1903 and soon proved Liberty right: several of the original *Tudric* designs were still in production in the 1920s.

The outstanding designer of *Tudric* was Archibald Knox (1864-1933), who had worked in Silver's studio in 1898. Knox's formalized plant forms and motifs were borrowed from medieval manuscripts and the *Book of Kells*, which were enjoying immense popularity at the time. Other designers of *Tudric* and *Cymric* are on the whole unknown personalities; many were young students in Birmingham working anonymously for the firm of William Haseler, the company responsible for the manufacture of the bulk of Liberty pewterware. Much has been made of this anonymity; some say identities were kept secret in order to stress the ideal of the medieval style of anonymous craftsmanship. But it is more likely that the firm of Haseler preferred to take the credit itself, rather than let it go to the individual designers. Nevertheless, the company produced quality objects that were precision molded, with their stylized decorations precise and clear. Inevitably though, the molds lost their clear definition, leading to the loss of detail that characterizes many of the later pieces. The *Tudric* and *Cymric* pieces are noteworthy not only for their fashionable Celtic and medieval motifs (as well as the more curvilinear styles to be found on the continent) but also for the combination of metals and other materials, such as wickerwork on the handles, enamels and semi-precious stones.

Earlier pieces were also finished by burnishing and hand-hammering. Areas of blue and green enamel colored the bright pewter –

bright because of its high silver content. A wide variety of products were made including decorative tableware, vases and desk sets. Complete tea and coffee services, which often retailed for as little as £6, made good design accessible to a wide public. This happy compromise between art and industry – the handcrafted appearance and the industrial production methods – enabled these wares to enjoy popularity long after Art Nouveau had ceased to be fashionable.

The English approach to the new age of the machine was seen by many artists and designers abroad as sound and sensible, and for many European designers it was epitomized by the metalwork of W A S Benson (1854-1924). Through his friendship with Edward Burne-Jones, Benson met William Morris, whom he had long admired, and was inspired to set up a workshop for the manufacture of metalwork in 1880. He later opened a well equipped factory in Hammersmith and, around 1887, a shop in Bond Street. Although he was a pupil and friend of Morris, an active member of the Art Workers' Guild from 1884 and a leader in the foundation of the Arts and Crafts Exhibition Society from 1886, even becoming chairman of Morris and Co after Morris's death in 1896, Benson was one of the few designers in the Art and Crafts circle who set out actively to use machines to mass produce his products. In brass and copper or in a combination of metals, Benson produced kettles, coat racks and electric lamps as well as some simple furniture, all designed with machine production in mind, using fine metal lines decoratively and also as structural supports. Exhibited at the opening of Bing's shop

RIGHT: *Archibald Knox employed interlacing Celtic knot motifs in this 'Tudric' pewter candlestick, made by the Silver Studios around 1905. The revival of interest in Celtic cultures and myths was the source of many of the motifs for British Art Nouveau designers.*

BELOW: *A 1902-03 'Tudric' pewter desk set, designed by Knox for Liberty and Co, shows the restrained curves of English Art Nouveau, a style that fell between the severe, rectilinear work of the Scottish and Viennese designers and the florid curvilinear forms of the French and Belgians.*

RIGHT: *This pewter rose bowl, designed by D Veazey for Liberty and Co in 1902, is inscribed with a line from Tennyson's poem* Maud: *'And the woodbine spices are wafted abroad and the musk of the rose is blown.' It is the last lines of the poem, however, that are better remembered: 'Come into the garden, Maud; For the black bat, night has flown.'*

BELOW RIGHT: *Molded honesty designs embellish this 'Tudric' tea service in pewter with cane handles, which was designed by Knox for Liberty and Co in 1903. A full service included a matching coffee pot and tray.*

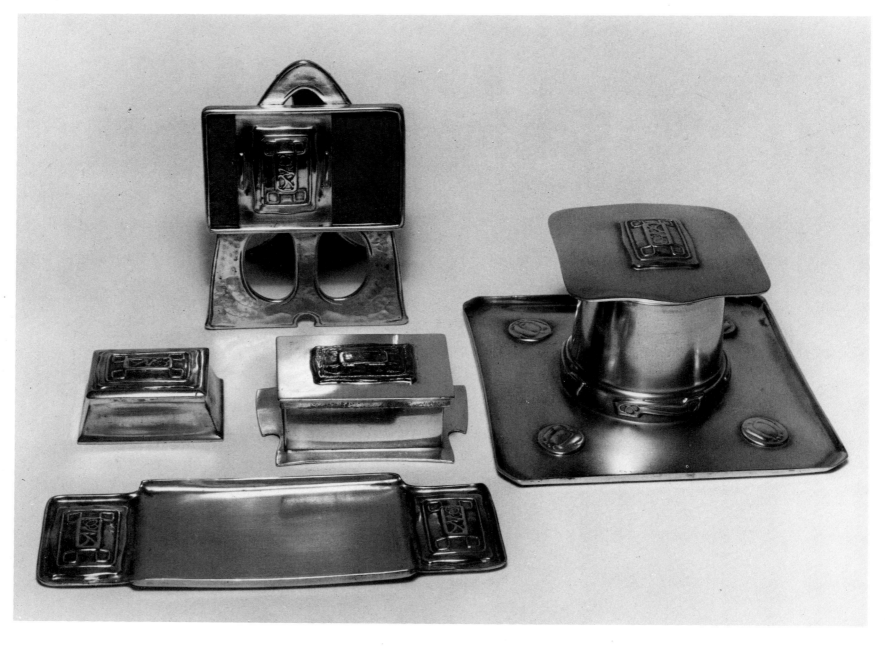

'L'Art Noveau' in December 1895, Benson's works, in particular his electrical fittings, were praised by Muthesias in *Dekorative Kunst* for their understanding of the mechanical process involved, but their shapes had still enough interest to encourage the fastidious Aubrey Beardsley to incorporate a Benson lamp in a caricature of fellow artist James McNeill Whistler.

Where Victorian metal and silverware was elaborately fussy and often overwrought, Art Nouveau works had a sophisticated fluidity to their lines. Art Nouveau designers freely used areas of undecorated metal to produce smoothness, while others exploited the metals' other qualities by hammering the surface to produce various textures. Scottish architect C R Mackintosh designed a range of flatware for use in Miss Cranston's tea rooms. Their attenuated shapes, characteristic of Mackintosh's preoccupation with the function of objects, give these pieces an almost abstract outline that prefigures modern Scandinavian designs of the twentieth century.

LEFT: *Silver cup and cover with enamel decoration designed by Archibald Knox (1899-1900).*

ABOVE RIGHT: *These examples of Liberty-style glass from around 1905 and, right, an aubergine vase from the mid-1920s, reflect the Art Nouveau taste for glassware set in pewter mounts.*

BELOW RIGHT: *Liberty and Co did not confine themselves to producing fine pieces in precious metals, but proved that good design in base metals could be equally stylish and popular. This copper 'log' box, with a repoussé lid and enamel medallion dates from around 1905.*

RIGHT: *With metalware such as this vase, Liberty and Co demonstrated that mass-production techiques did not necessarily produce poorly designed or low-quality goods.*

BELOW: *J P Kayser und Sohn of Cologne were the leading manufacturers of Art Nouvea pewterware in Germany. The success of their products such as this 1896 pewter tea service inspired Liberty to launch their 'Tudric' pewter range.*

RIGHT: *W A S Benson's work, such as this 1910 cane-handled silver kettle, won him the acclaim of Samuel Bing, in whose shop-cum-gallery 'L'Art Nouveau' his work was exhibited.*

BELOW: *This modern-looking silver flatware was designed by Josef Hoffmann for the* Wiener Werkstadt *around 1905.*

RIGHT: *Silver and painted casket by Josef Hoffmann and Carl Krenek (1910).*

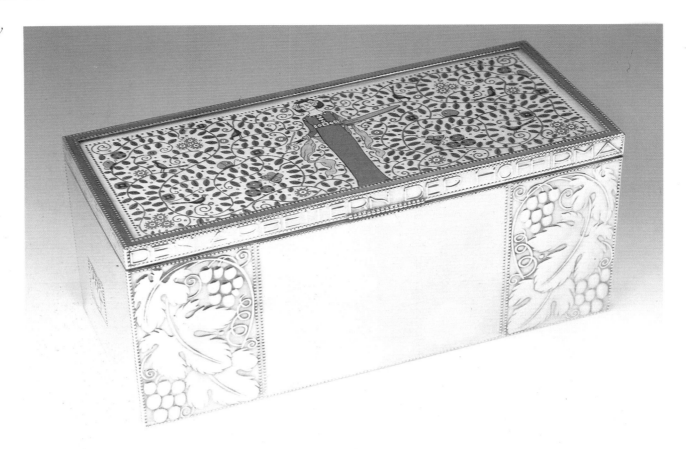

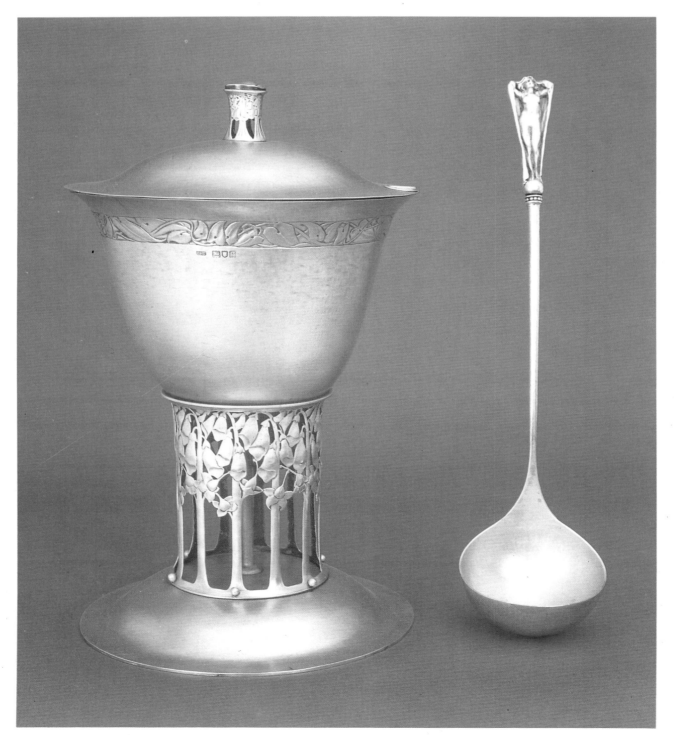

LEFT: *Where Victorian silverware was often highly wrought and elaborately fussy, Art Nouveau designers exploited the qualities of the metal by hand hammering the surface to provide textures, or by simply allowing areas of undecorated metal become part of the overall design. This 1902-03 Guild of Handicraft silver cup and cover and hammered silver ladle were designed by Charles Robert Ashbee.*

ABOVE: *This leaded peacock window, the work of an unknown designer around 1910, once lit the stairwell of a private house in Brighton.*

RIGHT: *The English image of women contrasts dramatically with that of European artists. On the continent, the archetypal Art Nouveau woman was the languid beauty or the femme fatale. English 'heroines,' such as the figure of Justice in this turn-of-the-century stained glass window by Morris and Co after a design by Burne-Jones, appear more war-like.*

Throughout the nineteenth century and even today, silversmiths continued to produce decorative candlesticks and candelabra despite the widespread introduction of electricity for domestic lighting. In the late 1890s electric lighting encouraged a fashion which would sweep America: no fashionable home was complete without a Tiffany or Tiffany-style lamp. The introduction of stained glass in electric lamp shades by Louis Comfort Tiffany (1848-1933) was perhaps one of his most significant contributions to functional commercial design. The multi-colored shade of textured glass softened the harsh light of incandescent bulbs and the later turgiten bulbs as well as concealing the often ugly electrical fittings. The most popular Tiffany lamps were based on plants and trees, but Tiffany was not content

simply to apply these motifs to the lamps. The plants and trees themselves 'became' lamps; bronze stems were transferred into trunks with tree roots spread out as the base, while the shades, irregularly shaped, hung as lily flowers, lotus flowers or wisteria blossoms.

Tiffany's father, Charles Louis Tiffany, had founded the firm of Tiffany and Young in 1837; by 1870, the name of Tiffany was synonymous with luxury and the firm acknowledged as America's finest outlet of jewelry and silverware, a fame later immortalized in Truman Capote's novel *Breakfast at Tiffany's*.

Despite the success of his father's business, Louis Tiffany preferred the fine arts and, as a student of George Innes, he developed into something of a romantic painter. After visiting Paris in 1868, Tiffany

LEFT: *The growth of electric lighting in the 1890s encouraged the fashion for Tiffany and Tiffany-style lamps. The most popular models were based on plant or tree forms, such as this Dragonfly lampshade on a turtle-back tile and mosaic base, made by Tiffany Studios.*

ABOVE LEFT: *'Laburnum' leaded glass and bronze table lamp, by Tiffany Studios.*

ABOVE RIGHT: *Bronze leaded glass and 'Favrile' glass table lamp by Louis Comfort Tiffany.*

LEFT: *'Zinnia' leaded glass, mosaic and bronze lamp, by Tiffany.*

LEFT: *Louis Comfort Tiffany designed this leaded glass window, depicting a Hudson River landscape, for the Beltzhoovers' house 'Rochroane' in New York in 1905. His other works in this vein included a glass screen for the White House.*

BELOW LEFT: *'Favrile,' a name Tiffany coined for wares such as this 1902 glass plate, was derived from the Latin* faber, *an artisan, and was intended to show that each piece was a unique art work.*

BELOW RIGHT: *Tiffany set up 'controlled accidents' to try and reproduce the color and textures of ancient and oriental glass in his collection. This 'Lava' vase, made around 1902, is set within a cast-bronze holder.*

traveled in Spain and North Africa where the Hispano-Moorish and Islamic art he saw deeply impressed him. Like so many of his generation, he also shared an interest in the Japanese art which was then being introduced into Europe. After acknowledging his shortcomings as a painter, Tiffany set himself up as a decorator in 1879 in partnership with Samuel Colman and Candace Wheeler. The major

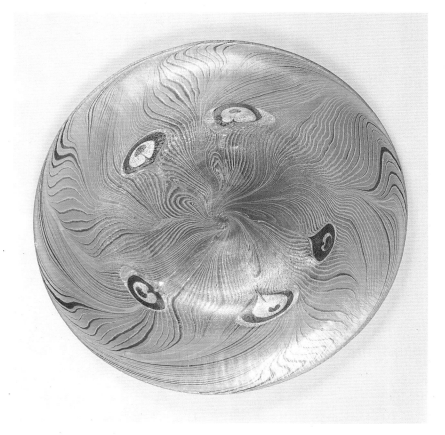

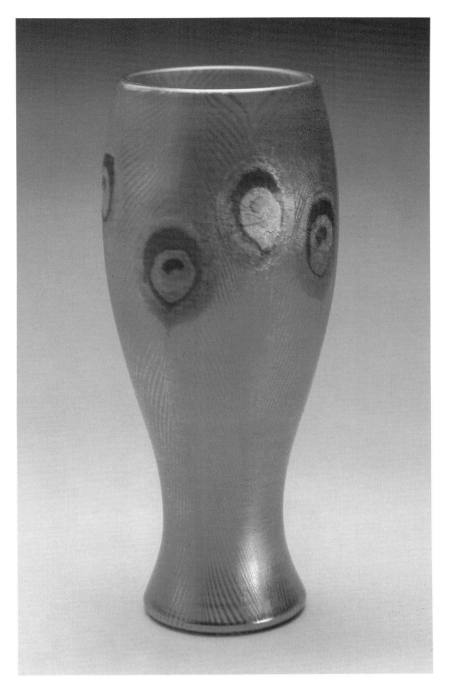

ABOVE LEFT: *The best-known and the most popular glassware produced by Tiffany was the Peacock ware.*

ABOVE RIGHT: *Tiffany's blown and manipulated 'Jack-in-the-Pulpit' vases proved to be the ideal shape for showing off his iridiscent glass. Of all the colors produced, peacock blue was the most popular.*

commission for the firm of Louis C Comfort and Associated Artists was for the redecoration of some of the rooms of the White House, including the manufacture of a magnificent glass screen.

In the mid-1870s Tiffany had become interested in glass-making techniques. This interest, by all accounts, grew into something of an obsession and led to the break up of his partnership. His collection of glass from the East and North Africa, with its freedom of form and often unintentional irregularity, appealed to Tiffany at a time when designers were attempting to escape from Western conventions. He was fascinated with the possibilities of incorporating decoration within the glass itself, and the iridescence of the antique glass he found on his travels inspired his best-known range of glassware, the gold and peacock lusterwares. During the centuries it had remained buried, the ancient glass had reacted with the surrounding soil, taking on an iridescent appearance. This natural process led Tiffany to set up 'controlled accidents' for his own glass.

In 1884 Tiffany re-formed his company as the Tiffany Glass Company. For ten years the firm concerned itself with experiments until, in 1894 it emerged as the Tiffany Glass and Decorating Company (which remained completely separate from the jewelry firm). In his so-called 'Jack in the Pulpit' vases, with their bulbous base with a long stem culminating in a large lily-like trumpet, Tiffany found the ideal shape to display the shimmering iridiscent effects he had perfected. The vases were made in a variety of colors, of which a rich peacock blue proved the most popular and effective. The increased demand for Tiffany's glassware led to the firm's expansion and ultimately to the production of some less inspired works. The commercial wares that were produced included harsh gold iridescent decorative tableware, but Tiffany continued personally to produce or closely super-

vise the production of fine quality special orders and experimental glass. Special-order glass pieces, such as rare red glass pieces whose color was obtained from compounds of gold, carried an engraved number. But almost all his glass had his name, or at least his initials, engraved upon it, with or without the trade name 'Favrile.' Tiffany derived the term 'Favrile' from the latin word *faber*, an artisan, to show that each piece was an individual work of art which could never be repeated or reproduced. Where some of Tiffany's glass has decoration of the utmost refinement, other pieces are pure experiments with the potentials of glass, lacking specific decorative elements. The 'Paperweight' vases use millefiori details to create the illusion of depth in the walls of glass. These employed a technique similar to that used in the manufacture of French paperweights, where finely extruded rods of different colored glass are embedded in the main body of the glass. Other glass pieces imitate stones, like the 'Agate' ware, or dripping lava and corroded textures. The elegant forms and decoration of many of Tiffany's products won the acclaim of Samuel Bing, who provided him with a European outlet.

Despite the fact that Tiffany had acquired followers in America, like the Quezal glass works in Brooklyn and art glass manufacturer Victor Durand in New Jersey, for most Americans Art Nouveau remained an exotic, and predominantly French, import.

LEFT: *Gallé firmly believed that glass need not be colorless and decorated by engraving alone. After experimenting, Gallé developed a variety of techniques for decorating 'within' the glass itself. This engraved glass vase was made by Gallé and designed by Victor Prouvé in 1888.*

RIGHT: *One technique developed by Gallé was* marqueterie sur verre, *where semi-molten glass was inserted into the body of a still-hot vase. This 'Pines' vase was made in 1903.*

BELOW LEFT: *Vase by Victor Durand, made at the Flint Glass Works in New Jersey (c 1925).*

BELOW RIGHT: *Iridiscent glass vases from Austria, by Professor R Bakalowits of Graz (c 1902).*

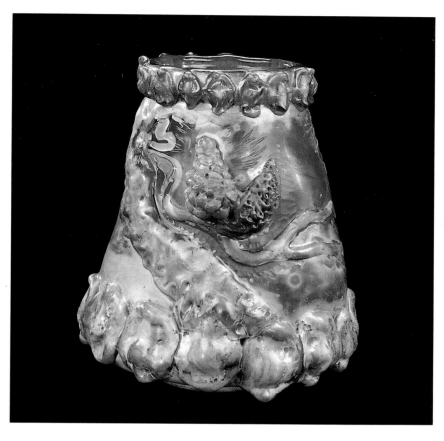

We are familiar with Emile Gallé as the designer of the fabulous Butterfly Bed, but he also produced glassware, and some of the most brilliant Art Nouveau pieces were made by his factory. In 1874 Gallé took over his father's firm and built it into possibly the largest manufacturer of luxury glassware in Europe. At the same time he pursued a course of experiments that resulted in a small output of works unrivaled in their invention. Gallé acknowledged nature as his greatest source of inspiration, and drew upon it for both the forms and decoration in his work. Gallé was convinced that glass was an infinitely variable medium that need not be simply clear and colorless, decorated only by engraving.

His initial experiments were confined largely to enameling on glass, but by 1884 he was coloring and decorating within the glass itself. At the Paris Exhibition of 1889 he displayed works in cameo glass and a technique he called *marqueterie sur verre*. This technique involved applying colored glass in a semi-molten state into the body of a still hot piece, which called for considerable skill and dexterity. Loyal to his native Lorraine, Gallé helped establish the *École de Nancy* which would rival Paris as a center for Art Nouveau production. His vases often contain decorations in the form of local flowers and trees, often are combined with lines of verse taken from the Symbolist poets.

LEFT: *After seeing Gallé's work exhibited in Paris, the Daum Brothers started producing carved and acid-etched vases such as these at their factory, the* Verrière de Nancy.

ABOVE: *The Daum Brothers used both cameo and internal decoration on this silver-mounted vase.*

RIGHT: *'Iris' vase (c 1895), by Gallé.*

By 1904 Gallé's factory was employing over three hundred people and had retail outlets in London, Paris and Frankfurt. The factory's most successful pieces were the newly popular table lamps in acid-etched cameo glass but the finest pieces from an artistic viewpoint were destined for exhibition or designed for a small circle of friends and wealthy patrons, which included the dandy Count Robert de Montesquiou and Marcel Proust.

Of all the glassmakers to be influenced by Gallé, perhaps the most important were the Daum brothers, August and Antonin. In 1875 their father had acquired a glass factory in Nancy, the Verriere de Nancy, where decorative table and domestic glassware was produced. After seeing Gallé's work exhibited in Paris, the Daum brothers turned their energies to producing art glass. The results, especially their cameo glass, were closely akin to Gallé's products, although the Daum brothers glass is distinctive in their use of mottled glass bodies and enameled decoration on acid-cut vases.

The career of René Lalique (1860-1945) spanned the last years of the nineteenth century and most of the first half of the twentieth. His ability to change his style to match the mood of the period allowed him to reign supreme as a leader of taste. Even more remarkable was his change of career: having trained as a jeweller, Lalique turned his attention to glass. Apprenticed at 16 to the jeweller Louis Auroc, Lalique went on to design for August Petit. In 1884 he formed a partnership with a friend, M Varenne, to market his jewelry designs. After an exhibition at the Louvre, Lalique's work attracted the attention of the jeweller Alphonse Fouquet, whose son Georges would later employ Alphonse Mucha. In 1885 Lalique opened his own workshop and began to work as a subcontractor to well-known firms such as Boucheron, Vever and Cartier. Five years later, he was employing over 30 assistants and began to design stage jewelry for Sarah Bernhardt. By this time he was using new and varied materials, mixing precious with non-precious materials, including glass, which was cast into stylized flowers or the heads of women. His fascination with the possibilities of vitreous enamels led him further in his experiments with glassmaking. From the early years of the twentieth century came Lalique's most notable vases, unique *cire perdue* (lost wax) pieces on which one can see the thumbmarks of the modeller reproduced in the glass.

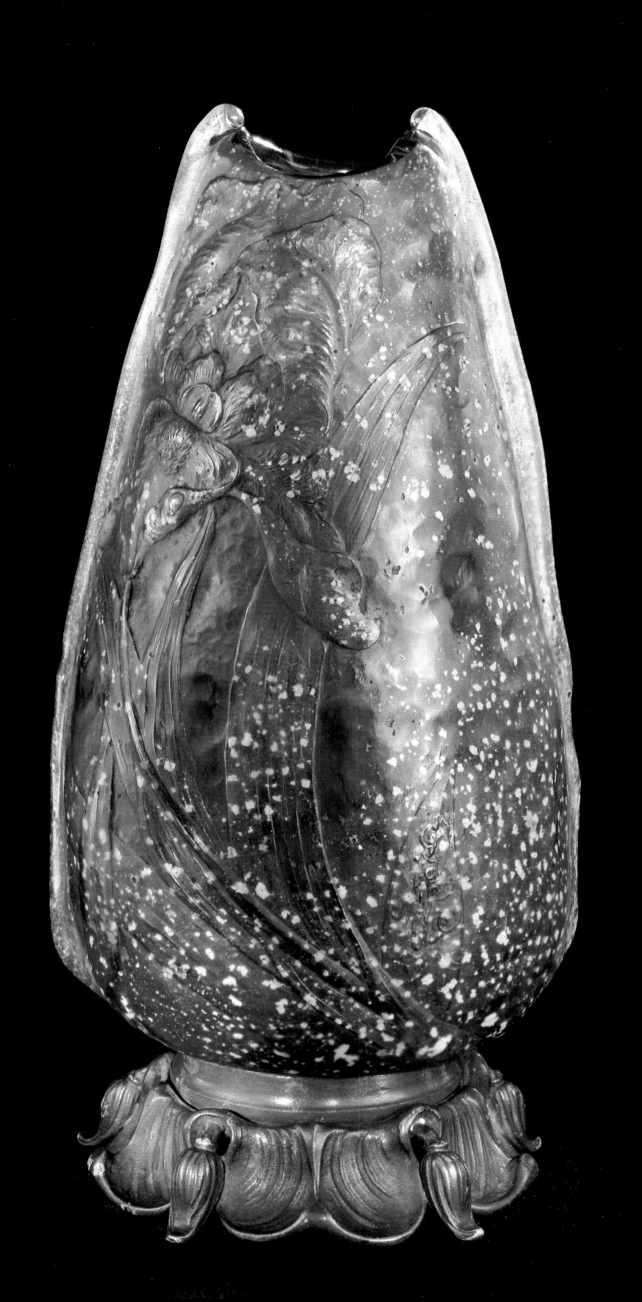

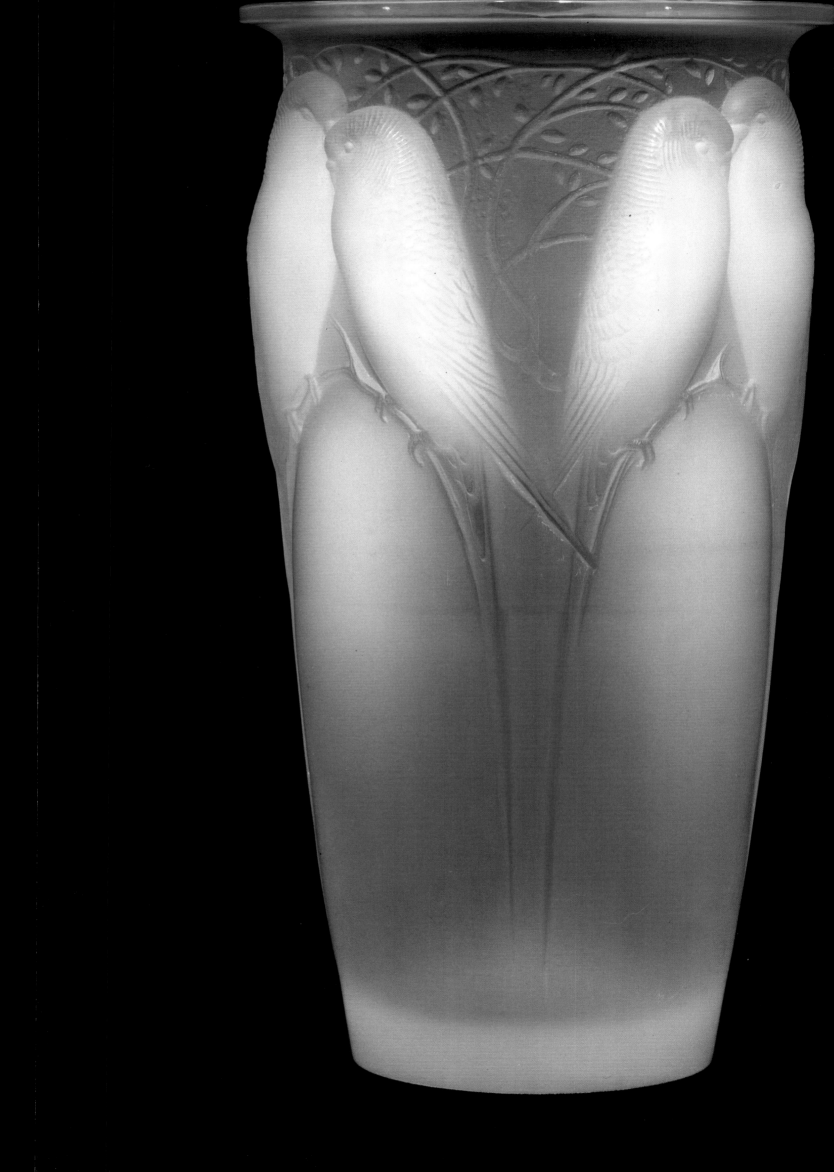

The turning point in his career came with a commission from the perfumier Francois Coty to design perfume bottles, which launched Lalique as a manufacturer of luxury and art glassware. Unlike Gallé and Tiffany, Lalique went no further with his experiments: his output remained limited to blue opalescent glass and colorless frosted or polished glass. Though many designs were available in a wide range of bright translucent colored glass, there was no internal decoration like that of Gallé and Tiffany. Instead, decoration was molded in relief or in intaglio, employing a graphic style that was sophisticated and distinctly Art Nouveau. The variety of goods that the Lalique factory produced was vast: vases, bottles, lamps, the famous motor car mascots, boxes and, of course, jewelry.

When porcelain was introduced in Europe in the early eighteenth century, the new material was so highly revered that national workshops were established, in particular in France and Germany. In the nineteenth century these workshops continued to produce ceramic wares in the same patterns that had been initially so popular. As a result, the outstanding pieces of the period are fabulous for their extreme intricacy and exaggeration, for as the ceramic and porcelain industries became complacent they also became less innovative.

In the last quarter of the nineteenth century a new generation of inspired artist-potters emerged. Keen to explore all the possibilities their art presented and urged on by the exhibitions of Chinese and Japanese wares, they abandoned the fussiness of the established style in favor of freedom of form and truth to materials. Exquisite works, such as the Copenhagen vase with its sea-holly motifs, were created in porcelain, but the craze was essentially for earthenwares. The medium was not only used for vases; it was modeled into figures. The swirling scarves and hair of dancer Loïe Fuller was one of the favorite images of modelers and sculptors, who extended and exaggerated the sweeping lines of her dress in clay.

Early exponents of Art Nouveau in ceramics in Hungary were the Vienna *Sezession* artists, including Vilmos Zsolnay (1828-1900). Zsolnay produced a number of pieces in strong Art Nouveau styles. Some of his pieces have flowers and women with flowing hair, modeled in full relief, while on others, linear Art Nouveau motifs are applied to vases. But it is his use of color that characterizes Zsolnay's work, particularly the repeated use of blues and reds shading to purple.

Alongside books and illustrations, the earliest – and some say the most important – vehicles of Art Nouveau abroad were textiles and wallpapers, including Mackmurdo's designs of the 1880s. It was in these lines that Liberty and Co were unsurpassed. Arthur Lazenby Liberty had prided himself on his imported Japanese fabrics and, on his return from Japan, opened a branch in the Avenue de l'Opéra to commemorate his success at the Paris Exhibition of 1889. The shop sold objets d'art and Liberty fabrics designed by Arthur Wilcox, Lindsay Butterfield and Arthur Silver, and these became a source of curvilinear motifs for continental artists and designers. As a result of the growing taste for simpler furnishings in the home, cotton and wool replaced silks and velvets. By the mid-1890s, when Silver was designing Liberty textiles, cotton had become associated with the image of country cottages and the simple (if idealized) rural lifestyle. Although cheap, Silver's fabrics were also sophisticated.

Victorian taste in wall coverings had favored 'all-over' patterns. The Art Nouveau interior designers preferred plain walls, to which decorative friezes were often added. The painter and illustrator Walter Crane (1845-1915) extended his repertoire to include a Lion and Dove Frieze design for Jeffery and Co, which was shown at the 1900 Paris Exhibition.

The Art Nouveau style in fabrics would not be confined to the textiles themselves: in the early years of the twentieth century, Liberty and Co issued a catalogue of what were called 'artistic' dresses, illustrated with color designs showing the wearer in a typical interior. In fact all the furniture and furnishings depicted could also be bought from Liberty's. The 'Amelia Evening Wrap' in muted blues and greens with hand-embroidered collar and cuffs reflected the fashion for Art Nouveau clothing. Even shoes would have the whiplash curve, the leitmotif of Art Nouveau, applied to them.

ABOVE LEFT: *'Omar' design for silk and wool double cloth (1898), by the architect of Great Warley Church, C H Townsend.*

ABOVE RIGHT: *Design for 'Isis' frieze by C A Voysey.*

LEFT: *'Pheasant and Rose' textile design (1896), by Walter Crane.*

Quite possibly the Art Nouveau objects that are most admired (and most coveted) are the fabulous pieces of jewelry designed by Lalique, Bing, Mucha and Tiffany, to name just a few. And it is in these pieces that Art Nouveau revealed an interest in a new type of woman. Where the image and ideal of Victorian womanhood was sober, virtuous, moral and conventional, the ideal Art Nouveau woman was the 'femme fatale,' a mysterious goddess whose splendor and beauty was to be glorified. The leaders of this revolutionary cult of womanhood

were themselves women: theater stars, dancers and celebrities, whose manners and dress were looked to for influence. Among them were the actress Sarah Bernhardt, who was also a sculptor and patron of the leading Art Nouveau artists, the American dancer Loïe Fuller, and Cléo de Mérode, a classically trained dancer who broke the rules by dancing with her hair loose and flowing and was called the most beautiful woman in France. And then there were the stars of the music hall, immortalized by Toulouse-Lautrec in his lithographs:

ABOVE: *A selection of Art Nouveau jewelry. The gold and opal ring is by A Knox and the gilt and luster glass brooch by Lalique.*

RIGHT: *A section of brooches, buckles and buttons by English, German, French and Scandinavian makers. The haircomb and parure de corsage are by Lalique.*

ABOVE RIGHT: *A gold and enamel pendant in the form of a woman's head, by Marcel Bing (c 1901)*

ABOVE: *L P Butterfield's 1896 watercolor sketch for a printed textile, 'Tiger Lily,' displays the Art Nouveau designer's love of floral patterns.*

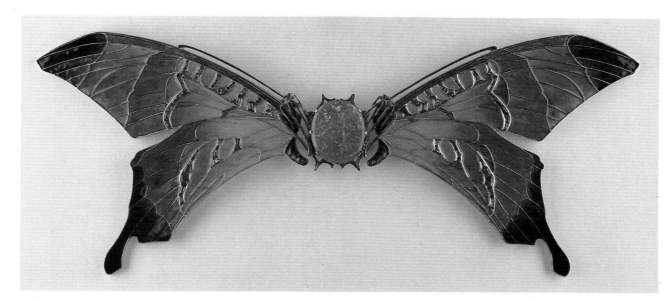

LEFT: *This gold and enamel buckle by René Lalique, set with sapphire and opal, takes the forms of two stylized swallowtail butterflies (1903-04).*

BELOW: *A gold and enamel pendant by Lalique features a low-relief profile of a young woman. Made between 1898 and 1900, it still has its original box.*

BOTTOM LEFT: *Georges Fouquet used* plique-a-jour *enamel and baroque pearls on this orchid flower brooch-pendant (c 1900).*

BOTTOM RIGHT: *This Lalique brooch-pendant uses the popular peacock form.*

Yvette Guilbert, Jane Avril and La Gouloue. Add to these public stars the famous courtesans of the 'demi-monde,' Liane de Pougy, Emiliene D'Alençon and Caroline Otéro, who between them amassed the most fabulous collection of Art Nouveau jewels, all gifts from their lovers and admirers. Where jewelry had in the past been created to adorn women, Art Nouveau jewelry celebrated woman, using her very image as the basis for designs.

Attitudes towards jewelry and its manufacture changed. Technical inventiveness became as important as inventive subjects. A variety of enamelling techniques were brought to bear, including *champ levé*, where the pattern is cut out of the surface of the enamel, *cloisonné*, where different colored enamels are separated by thin bands of metal, and *plique-à-jour*, where enamels are set like gems into a metal framework which has no back, allowing light to pass through the enamel so that it glows like a stained-glass window. The idea that jewelry was merely a setting for a precious stone was swept aside. Under the influence of Symbolist writings and Eastern mysticism, Art Nouveau designers became interested in semi-precious stones such as opals, moonstones and chrysoprase. As little importance was attached to the intrinsic values of the materials, designers were free to exploit misshapen stones, baroque and black pearls in their search for the unusual. Freely mixing their materials, French designers inclined towards the grotesque and fantastic: jewelry was made in the form of women's heads, nudes being swallowed by insects or metamorphosed into butterflies, their hair entwined with flowers. These extravagant curiosities appealed to a limited number of avant-garde customers, and the expensive and elaborate craftsmanship required to produce them depended on patronage.

Lalique and Georges Fouquet, who worked with Alphonse Mucha, enjoyed the patronage of Sarah Bernhardt. For Bernhardt's first night in the title role of *Cleopatra*, Fouquet translated Mucha's sketches into enamelled gold, carved ivory, pearls and semi-precious stones to create the famous Serpent Bracelet. (Evidently Miss Bernhardt had

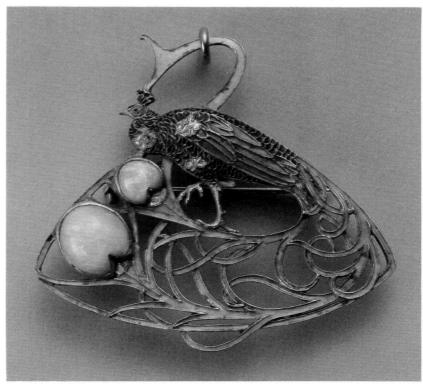

RIGHT: *Much English Art Nouveau silverware, such as this silver cup by C R Ashbee (1893), bears a strong resemblance to English ecclesiastical silver. The church was a major patron for such expensive metalware.*

LEFT: *Ashbee designed these mustard pots for the Guild of Handicrafts.*

RIGHT: *Silver belt buckle designed by Henri van de Velde.*

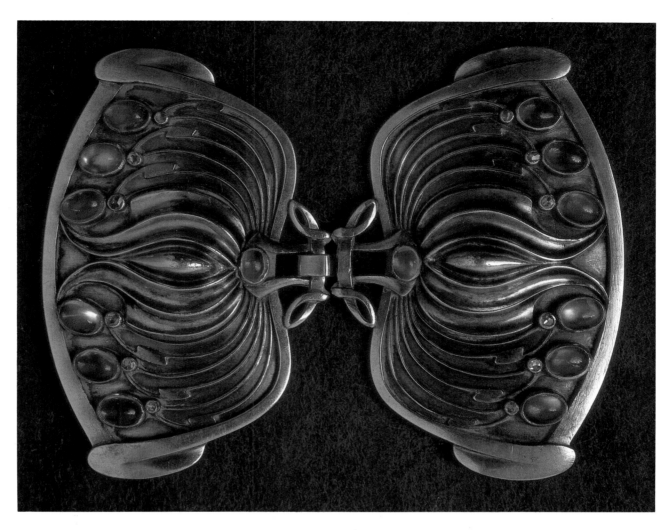

BELOW: *Left, hair comb by Gaillard (c 1900); top middle, hair ornament by Gautrait (c 1900); bottom middle, pair of clasps by Huber (c 1901); right, peacock brooch by C R Ashbee (c 1900).*

trouble paying for this jewel, and messengers were sent each night to claim a portion of the box office receipts.) Hearing of Lalique's talent, Bernhardt asked him to design jewels for her roles in *Izeyl* and *Gismonda*. The public acclaim that followed was enhanced when, at the Paris Exhibition of 1895, Lalique showed a piece of jewelry in the form of a female nude for the first time.

Where the French and Belgian jewellers such as Philippe Wolfers produced work that reflected the rarified, hot-house culture of the European Art Nouveau, with its synthesis of mysticism, symbolism and orientalism, British designers used comparatively understated natural motifs. Though they did not lack the skill, they lacked the customers and, to a great extent, the sexual freedom to produce jewels like their European counterparts. British Art Nouveau jewelry was still handmade, often created for wealthy patrons, and it is not surprising that some of the finest English jewelry was the result of ecclesiastical commissions.

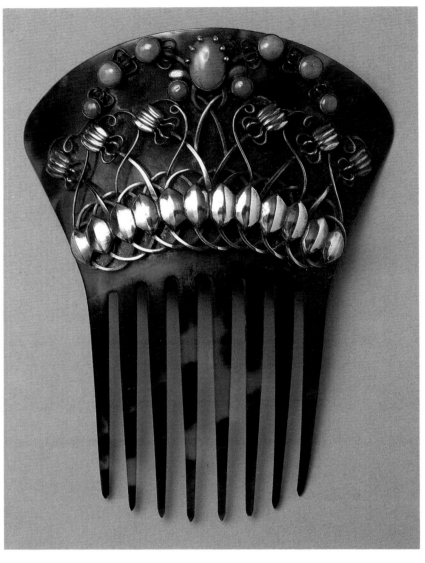

Charles Robert Ashbee worked in gold and silver, pearls, jade and turquoise to produce a pendant in the form of that popular subject for Art Nouveau fantasy, the peacock. Here, design is all important, for the gemstones are set within the metalwork rather than overwhelming it. The stones themselves reflect the expanding British Empire; the opals are from Australia, the pearls from India, the moonstones from Ceylon and the diamonds from South Africa. The pendant's subtle coloring and gentle luminosity contrasts strongly with the heavy, diamond-encrusted jewels of the Edwardian period. The most consistently attractive pieces of British Art Nouveau jewelry, however, are the buckles, pendants and brooches commissioned and sold by Liberty and Co: fine quality, reasonably priced silver-and-enamel pieces with semi-precious stones worked in abstract natural forms.

There are few examples of Art Nouveau earrings. The fashion for loose, flowing hair made them redundant; Art Nouveau women tended to prefer elaborate hair combs. There are, however, many fine gold chains culminating in pendants which could be detached and worn as brooches.

Contemporary journals encouraged British designers to work in silver instead of gold and to use enamel work in place of precious stones. After the 1900 Paris Exhibition, the more conventional types of jewelry in the Art Nouveau style were more or less mass produced, and the designers who made lasting commercial success were those, like Liberty in England and Jensen in Denmark, who adapted their designs to suit machine production.

LEFT: *Tortoiseshell and silver hair comb.*

BELOW: *Necklace by Haseler for Liberty and Co (1903).*

BELOW LEFT: *Pendant and chain by Ashbee for the Guild of Handicrafts (c 1903)*

RIGHT: *A selection of Art Nouveau jewelry; few earrings were made, as the fashionable long hair would have obscured them.*

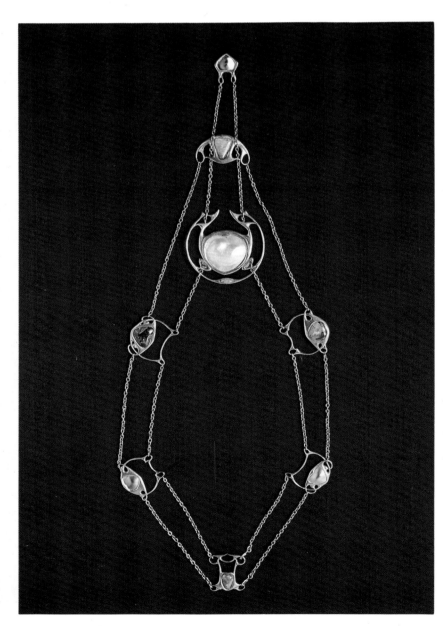

Architecture and Interior Design

LEFT: *A view of the west façade of Charles Rennie Mackintosh's Glasgow School of Art.*

Where the Arts and Crafts purists were distrustful of a conscious preoccupation with style and concerned themselves with ideological matters, the European Art Nouveau designers were concerned with the visual, and aimed to discover a new style for the twentieth century. And where the Arts and Crafts Movement aimed for honesty, simplicity and good craftsmanship, the Art Nouveau aimed for a sophisticated elegance which was often tinged with decadence.

The dictates of the Arts and Crafts movement allowed for a certain degree of flexibility when it came to the manufacturing of low-cost goods with little hand crafting, as long as the forms chosen were suitable for machine production. In architecture there was the question of how to use new materials like plate glass, steel and reinforced concrete. The problem was not so much how to build with these materials: the English and French engineers had successfully experimented in the construction of factories and exhibition halls. The real challenge was coming to terms with their use, deciding how the materials should be displayed, internally and externally, and how far the new materials should suggest new architectural forms.

Art Nouveau has been credited with changing the tradition of adapting new materials to existing styles, freeing steel and glass from their secondary role as well as exploring and exploiting their decorative possibilities.

In most cases, a building is called Art Nouveau because of its ornaments, yet Art Nouveau architecture can be found without Art Nouveau decoration. Some of the qualities of Art Nouveau decoration, such as curving lines and a lack of symmetry, are less suited to architecture simply because buildings, on the whole, have to be functional and their construction requirements make it difficult to create curving whiplash forms as exteriors.

Despite these considerations, some of the most potent examples of Art Nouveau that remain today are buildings. In some, many of their original interior fittings survive: others have lost their original interiors but their exteriors for the most part remain with their character intact.

As in the other fields of design, the Art Nouveau style permeated buildings with a wide variety of functions: public houses and churches, underground stations, art galleries and theaters as well as commercial buildings and private houses. Some reflect the curvilinear mode of Art Nouveau in their decorative details and biomorphic forms, others the rectilinear mode in their clear lines and straight edges. *Punch*, always aware of the latest fashions and movements in

art, was quick to lampoon the new style. R C Carter's cartoon *The Home Made Beautiful* (1903) made an unfavorable comparison between the austere nature of Art Nouveau furnishings and their cosily

TOP: *Art Nouveau lettering in the London underground station at Edgware Road.*

ABOVE: *This tiled ticket office window at Edgware Road underground station offers a more restrained English answer to Guimard's Métro station entrances.*

THE LATEST STYLE OF ROOM DECORATION. THE HOME MADE BEAUTIFUL.

According to the " Arts and Crafts."

LEFT: *Although* The Home made Beautiful *by R C Carter, from a 1903 issue of* Punch, *is clearly intended as a lampoon, the cartoon is nevertheless an accurate description of Art Nouveau furnishings.*

ABOVE: 'The Black Friar,' a public house in the Art Nouveau style, is one of the finest examples of a commercial building in the style in London. The Black Friar takes its name from the former Dominican Friary whose site it occupies.

ABOVE RIGHT: The colors of 'The Black Friar's' external decorations – greens, blues and golds – are found again inside, enriched by some of the most remarkable Art Nouveau stained glass outside of religious buildings.

RIGHT: Mosaic decoration over entrance to the saloon of 'The Black Friar'. The façade, stained glass, interiors and marble slabs carved in low relief were all the work of Henry Poole.

stuffed Victorian equivalents. At the same time, the cartoon made a subtle comment on the new-found status of women; the Art Nouveau furnishings clearly reflect her taste and not that of her husband.

Possibly one of the most comfortable views of the new style is from inside 'The Black Friar,' a public house at Blackfriars on the site of a Dominican Friary dissolved by Henry VIII. The marble slabs,

ABOVE: *Holy Trinity Church in Sloane Street, London was designed by J D Sedding; his assistant Henry Wilson designed the railings. Inside, the great east window was designed by Burne-Jones and made by William Morris.*

RIGHT: *As the twentieth century advanced, the Art Nouveau style in England became mixed with a variety of others. The Willing House in Grays Inn Road, London, designed by Hart and Waterhouse, is a fine example of this eclectic approach.*

decorated with low relief bronze figures by Henry Poole, would not look out of place in a church, but the color scheme of the stained glass, predominantly green, blue and gold, gives an effect more submarine than celestial. For that quality of light, one need only visit Holy Trinity Church in Sloane Street, London, where it is provided by the great east window designed by Edward Burne-Jones and made by William Morris. Holy Trinity was designed by J D Sedding and completed after his death by his assistant Henry Wilson (1864-1934), who also designed the iron railings that separate the forecourt of the church from the street. Inside, enclosing the choir stalls are cast-bronze panels, designed by F W Pomeroy, of angels carrying scrolls.

Number 37 Harley Street, London, is another interesting example of Art Nouveau in England. It was rebuilt in 1899 in Monk Park stone by Beresford Pite with decorative panels by the sculptor F E Schenck, portraying the arts and sciences. As the twentieth century advanced, the Art Nouveau style in England would become mixed with a variety of other styles: the Willing House in Grays Inn Road, London, is a good example of the mix. Designed by architects Hart and Waterhouse, many traces of Art Nouveau have nevertheless survived.

Jeweler and silversmith Charles Robert Ashbee (1863-1942) was also responsible for the design of buildings and interiors. His own house at 39 Cheyne Walk, London, displayed the Art Nouveau style – even if the familiar curves are absent – particularly in the relationship between the horizontal, small-paned windows and the 'negative' spaces between them. The interiors were decorated throughout by the Guild of Handicrafts, using tooled leather wall coverings in some areas, and became the subject of illustrated articles in *The Studio* in 1895, and by Hermann Muthesias in *Dekorative Kunst* in 1898.

In 1897 the Grand Duke of Hesse had sent a special envoy from Darmstadt to see Ashbee's work. The result of these enquiries would lead to W H Baillie Scott's commission to decorate and furnish the

ABOVE: *Number 39, Cheyne Walk, Chelsea was designed by silversmith and jeweler Charles Robert Ashbee, and is a showpiece of Guild of Handicraft workmanship.*

BELOW: *Number 37, Harley Street, designed by Beresford Pite, has decorative panels by F E Schenk.*

Grand Duke's Palace with pieces like the Music Cabinet (1898). Further commissions followed and through these, the magazines and European exhibitions, Ashbee and the Guild of Handicrafts would inspire Josef Hoffmann's workshops in Vienna, thereby spreading the Art Nouveau style abroad.

With the passing of time, the effects of war and the rebuilding of exteriors, many fine examples of Art Nouveau buildings have been lost. But often, by looking at the upper parts of buildings, we can still find fine examples of the style. The Apollo Theatre on Shaftesbury Avenue, London, was designed in 1900, the year of the Paris exhibition where, under the *Porte Monumental*, lit by incandescent lamps, artists would meet. Designed by Lewin Sharp and opened in 1901 with an appropriate production, *The Belle of Bohemia*, the façade shows the 'belles' of the turn of the century as well as angled windows set into cartouches.

The most remarkable building designs in England during the Art Nouveau period belong to C Harrison Townsend (1852-1928) whose principal works are the Whitechapel Art Gallery dating from 1897-99 and the Horniman Museum of 1900-02. In the first, the building betrays a variety of sources: the asymmetry of the ground floor in relation to the upper floor and the leaf ornamentation belong to H H Richardson (1838-1886), who helped the United States to make its claim for the lead in the vanguard of architecture. In the second building, a mural decorates the façade, in front of which stands the square clock tower with its straight edges rounded off.

In spite of these outstanding examples, the main British – as opposed to the purely English – achievements in Art Nouveau are the buildings and furnishings of the Scotsman Charles Rennie Mackintosh (1868-1928), one of the new generation of European architects who sought to establish a national architecture.

ABOVE: *The Whitechapel Art Gallery, by C Harrison Townsend, dates from 1897 to 1899.*

LEFT: *The interiors of Townsend's church at Great Warley were designed by Sir William Reynolds-Stephens. The vaulting is traversed by ribbons of aluminum, with plates of aluminum decorated with embossed lilies inserted into the walls. The entire vaulting of the apse is clad in aluminum sheets decorated with bright red bunches of grapes. Great Warley Church is one of England's rare extant examples of Art Nouveau architecture and interior design.*

RIGHT: *The Horniman Museum, with its distinctive clock tower, was built by Townsend between 1900 and 1902. The museum was designed to contain the collection of the Horniman family, whose wealth had been amassed through tea shipping.*

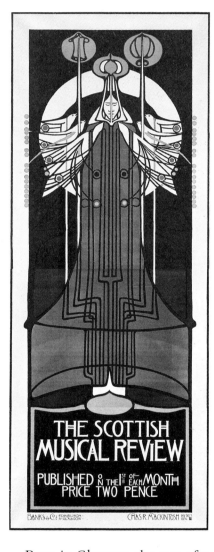

Born in Glasgow, the son of a police superintendent, Mackintosh began his career in 1884 as an apprentice to local architect John Hutchinson and enrolled in evening classes at the Glagow School of Art where, in line with the rest of British architectural education, the belief was that architecture was an art of adornment. But since the 1870s there had been a great interest in Glasgow in the arts, focused on a group of young painters who became known as the Glasgow School. And when Francis Newbery became head of the Glasgow School of Art, bringing with him a direct knowledge of artistic developments in London, the school became one of the finest in Britain and attracted much attention from the rest of Europe.

After completing his articles, Mackintosh joined the firm of Honeyman and Keppie where he became friendly with fellow draftsman H J MacNair. By 1892 Mackintosh had developed a fully Art Nouveau decorative style which utilized aspects of elongation and abstraction, a style much influenced by the appearance in 1893 of the magazine *The Studio* which contained illustrations of the works by Voysey, Beardsley's illustrations for Wilde's play *Salomé* and the Java-born Dutch symbolist Jan Toorop's painting called *The Three Brides*. Around the same time, Newbery had noticed a similarity of style in the work of Mackintosh and MacNair to that of two sisters, Margaret and Frances

Macdonald, and the four designers were brought together. The Four, as they became known, developed a common style, designing metalwork and posters such as Mackintosh's severely rectilinear poster for the *Scottish Musical Review* which attracted criticism for its abstraction when it was shown in 1896 at the Arts and Crafts Exhibition.

Having become a partner at Honeyman and Keppie in 1894, Mackintosh received his first important commission as a freelance designer in 1897: the new Art School in Glasgow, which was built between 1898 and 1899 and extended between 1907 and 1909. This commission would be followed closely by the first of the tea rooms for Miss Cranston.

Through his education within the mainstream of the Gothic Revival, Mackintosh learned a craft approach to building. This and Lethaby's book *Architecture, Mysticism and Myth* (1892) helped to bridge the distance between Celtic mysticism and the Arts and Crafts' approach to form. Mackintosh had always taken the more traditional approach, derived from Ruskin, which argued that modern materials like iron and glass could not replace stone because they lacked 'mass.' In the new Glasgow School of Art, despite the wealth of local gray granite and roughcast brick, iron and glass would be present in large quantities. The school, the result of a competition, was built in

LEFT: *The north façade of the Glasgow School of Art. The projecting iron brackets, bent back against the windows like stylized flowers, are both decorative and functional as they provide support for window cleaners' planks.*

ABOVE: *The east staircase of the Glasgow School of Art, at the first floor level.*

ABOVE RIGHT: *The Library at the Glasgow School of Art belongs to the second phase of building, from 1907 to 1909.*

two stages and is a record of Mackintosh's stylistic development from 1896 to 1909.

The competition was initiated by Mackintosh's friend, tutor and patron Francis Newbery. His schedule proved too demanding for the budget of £14,000, so the competitors were asked to design a two-stage building, with the first stage to be constructed under the specified sum. The design that Mackintosh submitted on behalf of Honeyman and Keppie was not a fixed or final plan, but served Mackintosh as an 'intention' which was subject to refinements and improvements during the course of the building program. But in the first place it was the actual site that determined many of the characteristics of the building. This was a long, narrow rectangle of land lying east to west on the south side of the main, highly sloping access road. Newbery's demands for the school consisted of functional specifications such as large studios with uninterrupted north light and adequate heating.

The result was a plan rather like the letter E, with a series of studios connected by corridors. Despite the logical symmetry offered by the plan, Mackintosh utilized deliberately asymmetrical aspects: the huge studio windows reflect the various sizes of the rooms behind them, resulting in a non-uniform exterior bay spacing. The asymmetrical balance is continued further in the treatment of the entrance bay with the offset door and small window. But the railings, precisely

symmetrical to the front entrance, show that the entrance door, despite its initial off-set appearance, is in fact at the physical center of the façade. The entrance door and surround were altered later to give them a more Art Nouveau form along with the gate pillars, topped by stylized clumps of tulips and an ironwork arch. One feature of the exterior which never escapes mention is the use of projecting iron brackets on the studio windows. Characteristic of Mackintosh's later decorative work, they are also a functional necessity: they support window cleaners' planks. The decorative heads of the brackets give relief to the expanses of glass and appear rather like flowers bent against the windows.

A more conventional use of ornament, however, is illustrated by the sculpted motif over the main entrance, whose curves blend into the molding around the doorway. While the exterior walls of the school are in local granite, the internal structure is based on brick piers with steel girders for the widest spans and cast-iron beams for smaller ones. The size of the interior spaces could be changed by removing the wooden partitions separating each studio. In the sub-basement Mackintosh incorporated an effective ducted heating and ventilation system, served by a large fan-room next to the boiler room and fed by fresh-air grilles beside and below the main entrance. The main heating duct supplied the vertical branches built into the corridor walls; these branches opened into the studios themselves by a series of grilles.

In the first phase of the building from 1897 to 1899, two rooms indicate the direction in which Mackintosh's style was moving: the original Board Room in the east wing (which now houses a permanent exhibition of the School's collection of Mackintosh's furniture, drawings, paintings and models) and the Directors' Office. Every detail of the rooms – every chair, table, clock and each piece of cutlery – was designed in relation to its setting. Both rooms are 'white rooms': in the Board Room the steel beams spanning the ceiling are left exposed but painted white, and in the Directors' Room, the apartment is panelled all round to a height of eight feet with built-in cupboards and panels of decorative leaded glass.

LEFT: *The* Room de Luxe *at the Willow Tea Rooms in Sauchiehall Street, Glasgow, designed for Miss Cranston, 1902-04. The gesso panel was designed by Margaret Macdonald Mackintosh.*

RIGHT: *For Miss Cranston's Tea Rooms at Buchanan Street, Mackintosh designed the mural in patterns of roses and women in a style derived from his own posters.*

If these two rooms are the show pieces of the first phase of building, the finest room of the second phase is undoubtedly the Library, and it is here that the angular style, with its passion for straight lines, is displayed. The Library remains basically as it was indicated in the plans of 1896: thirty-five feet square and seventeen feet high, with an open gallery running around the upper part of the room, creating a rectangular well within the square. The gallery itself is set back on beams about three feet from the supporting pillars, and the space between is filled by scalloped balusters which have their concave facets painted in alternating bright colors. Alternate panels of the gallery front drop as slightly convex pendants and are carved in a series of abstract patterns, each one different and offering subtle differences in reflected light. In the center of the room is a pendant cluster of pierced metal lampshades whose design is repeated in single lamps arranged throughout the Library. Thirteen hanging lamps, each looking like a small skyscraper, are made of brass and zinc and are screened with colored glass. A circular hole in the white-painted

inner reflector allows light to pass down through the lower part of the outer, pierced copper shades. The whole interior of the Library has been called a masterpiece of spatial composition: externally the windows climb almost from the pavement to light its three storeys.

Further opportunities to explore the potentials of interior design were provided by Miss Catherine Cranston, one of Mackintosh's most sympathetic clients, both in her own house Hous'hill and in her series of tea rooms established in the center of Glasgow at the turn of the century. The tea rooms themselves were something of a social phenomenon which grew out of an enthusiasm for non-alcoholic refreshment rooms and as a place where Edwardian ladies could properly meet without their chaperones.

At the time of their meeting, Miss Cranston had two premises, at Buchanan Street and Argyle Street, undergoing structural and decorative changes in readiness for opening. The tea rooms had more to them than their name suggests: there were, in addition, luncheon rooms, billiard rooms and smoking rooms. In 1897, in conjunction

RIGHT: *Detail of the mural by
Mackintosh for the Buchanan
Street Tea Rooms. The
predominant colors of the scheme
were reds and purples, fashionable
in both interior and textile design.*

FAR RIGHT: *White furniture and
lamp fittings designed by
Mackintosh.*

BELOW: *Simple lines and dark
stains rather than varnishes were
the hallmarks of many of
Mackintosh' designs such as this
chair.*

BELOW RIGHT: *White chair designed
by Mackintosh and exhibited at the
Turin Exhibition in 1902.*

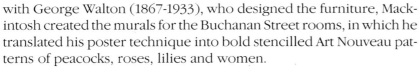

with George Walton (1867-1933), who designed the furniture, Mackintosh created the murals for the Buchanan Street rooms, in which he translated his poster technique into bold stencilled Art Nouveau patterns of peacocks, roses, lilies and women.

In the next project for the Argyle Street rooms, Mackintosh's contribution was limited once more, but this time to the design of the furniture. From 1894 Mackintosh was most active designing furniture. Several pieces were for the general market, while others were commissioned by the Glasgow firm of cabinetmakers Guthrie and Wells. The furniture was simple, the rectangularity relieved in places by a long sweeping curve, strap hinges and fittings. Avoiding the use of varnish, Mackintosh preferred dark green and brown stains which resulted in a quality that was close to the pieces produced by the Arts and Crafts designers. The difference, however, lay in Mackintosh's

tendency to refine the structural pieces in his furniture, making them more slender and delicate in contrast to the homely chunkiness of the English pieces.

Mackintosh is known to have been concerned with the introduction of vertical elements within an interior: he disliked the idea of all the furniture being too much the same height. Some of the verticals of the chair backs would rise above the most elaborately dressed hair and feather hats, while other chairs had their back supports curtailed abruptly. These very low-backed chairs are said to have been used by Miss Cranston's waitresses during less busy periods in the tea rooms. By present-day standards, the chairs are uncomfortable after a long period, but it must be remembered that these chairs were not designed for relaxing in, but for sitting upright with the correct Edwardian deportment.

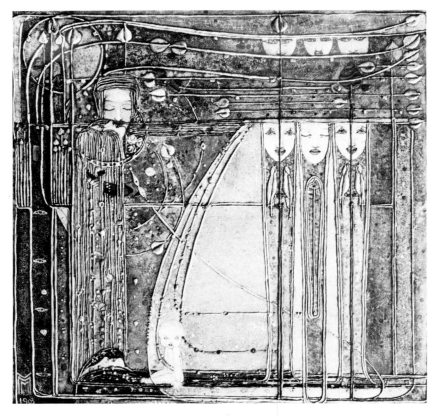

After 1901 Mackintosh had sole control of the design of Miss Cranston's tea rooms at new premises in Ingram Street, and from 1902 to 1904 at the Willow Tea Rooms in Sauchiehall Street. The Willow Tea Rooms were housed in a building also designed by Mackintosh, and featured five tea salons, a dining gallery and a billiard room. In these rooms, Mackintosh's use of symbolism is most apparent: the whole of the Willow Tea Rooms were decorated with a willow-leaf motif and abstracted forms in the plaster and ironwork relating to tree shapes. Both the name and the motif were appropriate as the street name, Sauchiehall, was itself derived from 'willow.'

The Room de Luxe was painted white with a dado above which, on three sides, was a mural made of mirror-glass panels. On one wall, a gesso panel by Margaret Macdonald Mackintosh (the couple had married in 1900, a year after MacNair married Margaret's sister, Frances) based on Rossetti's Sonnet 'O all ye that walk in willow wood.' The Room de Luxe survives in part, though without Mackintosh's furniture, as the coffee room of Daly's Department Store. The doors and window were of leaded glass with the dominant colors of purple and rose, with a remarkable chandelier made of glass bubbles. The effect of the white interiors and furniture offset by the colors in the stained glass panels and doors captivated Mackintosh's European admirers: the Willow Tea Rooms were illustrated in 1905 in the German magazine *Dekorative Kunst* and followed the Four's exhibition of white rooms at the Vienna *Sezession* Exhibition in 1900 and the Turin Exhibition in 1902.

A main source of information regarding Mackintosh's work in domestic interiors and furnishings, since many of its contents have survived, is Hill House in Helensburgh, built for publisher W W Blackie. In Mackintosh's own writings and at Hill House itself, it is possible to see the legacy of the Scottish Baronial buildings which fascinated him and were to influence his designs. Built in local stone with traditional construction techniques, the building's elements are arranged according to their function, not their appearance. Externally, taking account of Scottish rains that are blown horizontally as well as falling vertically, the walls rise to protect the gable ends of the roof. Internally the irregularity of the rooms is derived from their use. The living room has two recesses, one a bay projecting from the face of the building, with a built-in seat and two doors which lead into the garden. At this, the 'summer' end of the room, there is a concentration of light which contrasts with the 'winter' end of the room with its fireplace and small window. The second recess was designed to hold the family's piano. The white walls of the room rise to the height of the bay window; above the picture rail, both walls and ceiling are painted dark, with the result that the main area of the room is established.

ABOVE LEFT: *The Opera of the Wind, a decorative panel for the Warndorfer Music Room in Vienna by Margaret Macdonald Mackintosh. Fritz Warndorfer would later become the financial backer of the Wiener Werkstadt.*

LEFT: *The main bedroom at Hill House in Helensburgh, designed by Mackintosh for the publisher W W Blackie. The main height of the room is established by the furniture set into recesses.*

In the main bedroom, the bed is positioned in a large barrel-vaulted alcove off the main rectangle of the room. Again heights are established by the use of wardrobes, which are placed in recesses as deep as the furniture and which rise up as high as the top of the windows. Thus the arches and walls flow almost organically into each other, complemented by the varying verticals of the furniture.

After 1900 Mackintosh's name was widely celebrated abroad, though his work was little known in England. In Europe, he was fêted by Josef Hoffmann, and in 1901 the *Sezession* magazine *Ver Sacrum* was devoted to Mackintosh's work. This led Mackintosh to enter a competition organized by Alexander Koch's magazine *Zeitschrift für Innin-Dekoration* to design a house for an 'art lover.' Although Mackintosh strayed from the competition rules, he was considered important enough to merit a special award. In 1902, Mackintosh was commissioned to design a music room in Vienna for Fritz Warndorfer, who became the financial backer of the *Wiener Werkstadt* in the following year.

In 1903 Mackintosh's work became known in Russia: examples of his designs were illustrated in the avant-garde *Mir Iskusstva* (The World of Art) and in 1905, 35 illustrations of Hill House appeared in *Deutsche Kunst und Dekoration*.

But at home, Mackintosh's work received little publicity, and in 1914 he left Glasgow for good. After moving to London, he received no architectural commissions. Isolated from his strongest supporters in Austria and Germany by the war, Mackintosh found his career in decline. Coupled with his habitual heavy drinking, this lack of recognition led to his death in poverty in 1928.

Mackintosh occupies a unique position in the history of the modern movement: in his work he took what he needed from his Scottish background, from the Arts and Crafts movement and from Art Nouveau, and brought them together in his own personal style. While his buildings and furniture may appear forward looking, Mackintosh was entrenched in the nineteenth century: while he was denying the possibilities of steel and glass taking the place of stone in architecture, Louis Sullivan had completed his Carson, Pirie and Scott Store in Chicago. And despite the similarities between Mackintosh's work and the Viennese designers such as Hoffmann and Olbrich, by looking at the Scot's work alongside those of his contemporary French or Belgian Art Nouveau designers, the essential differences are apparent.

ABOVE: *Mackintosh's 'Art Lover's' House earned him an award in Koch's 1901 competition.*

BELOW: *Chairs designed for Hill House by Mackintosh. The severity of Mackintosh's rectilinear style has recently enjoyed a revival.*

ABOVE: *Mackintosh's sketch for the* Daily Record *Buildings.*

RIGHT: *The* Castel Béranger *apartment building was designed by Hector Guimard for Madame Fournier. Separating the 'service' stairs at the rear from the main staircase inside is a wall of double curved glass tiles. The glass wall allows light to pass from the rear of the building through to the main stairs without the intrusion of servants or tradesmen.*

RIGHT: *Hector Guimard's Métro station entrances, such as this one at Abbesses, used prefabricated sections of cast iron. Between 1900 and 1904, 140 such entrances were built in Paris.*

BELOW: *Guimard's cast-iron sections were painted green to resemble bronze. Despite their sinuous and delicate appearance the entrances have stood nearly a hundred years of constant use. Even the typography is treated in the same flowing style.*

As the curvilinear mode of Art Nouveau developed, the features that had first been used by Mackmurdo in his title page for *Wren's City Churches* and again in his fretwork-backed chair and textile designs, became more apparent. The sinuous flowing lines were capable both of decorating solid forms and being used structurally. Thus the ideals of beauty and utility could be married, as they were by Hector Guimard (1867-1942) in his plant-like, arched cast-iron Paris Métro station entrances.

Guimard, one of the best-known French Art Nouveau architects, received a traditional academic education at the École des Beaux-Arts in Paris from 1885 to the early 1890s. While studying there he became acquainted with the theories of Eugène-Emmanuel Viollet-le-Duc (1814-1879) who, like the Arts and Crafts Movement, advocated the essential unity of the arts. Having won a scholarship, Guimard was able to visit England and Scotland to study the works he had read about in magazines. Although impressed by what he saw, he was more influenced by his visit to Belgium to see the architect Victor Horta (1861-1947), who had designed his *Hôtel Tassel* in 1892.

In 1894 Guimard was commissioned to design a block of apartments in Paris, the *Castel Béranger* for Madame Fournier. Guimard drew up plans in a neo-Gothic style in 1895, but in the year he met Horta, so the story goes, he was persuaded to forget the 'flower' and concentrate on the 'stem.' Returning to Paris, Guimard completely redesigned the *Castel Béranger*, introducing several new features. Each of the 38 apartments was to have an individual plan, making them varied and irregular. This same varied and irregular quality is evident once more in the façade. For this, Guimard used a variety of materials: brick, carved stone, wrought iron, cast terracotta, iron and bronze. In the façade, we see all the characteristics of the curvilinear mode of Art Nouveau: asymmetry, the predominance of line, and ornamentation that is structural and in certain cases functional. Many of the building's features were the result of Guimard's idea of being both artist and master of works; he undertook all aspects related to his architecture, including the ironwork, stained glass, ceramics, carpets and even the lettering.

RIGHT: *The glass-topped dome of Horta's Hôtel Van Eetvelde is supported by steel stanchions and decorated with stained glass. The dome lights the central living space of the house.*

BELOW: *With the Hôtel Tassel (1892-93), Victor Horta became one of the first architects to make extensive use of iron in a domestic building.*

Like his mentor Victor Horta, Guimard was prepared to expose iron and glass where necessary. At the top of the building are rarely seen iron details that resemble sea horses, while at the back of the building, separating the main staircase from the service stairs, is a wall of double curved glass panels in alternating shapes. But it is the famous iron entrance gate that most clearly expresses the Art Nouveau style in its asymmetrical balance of swirls and straight lines.

Guimards' Métro station entrances date from 1900 to 1904. One hundred and forty entrances were built in Paris, many of which survive today. Important not only as examples of Art Nouveau, the station entrances are significant in their use of prefabricated cast-iron elements, for Guimard believed that modern machine methods should be used whenever possible. The cast iron was painted green to resemble bronze, and although they may appear intricate in design, the entrances have stood up well to the strain of three quarters of a century's heavy use. Guimard even treated the typography and lighting in the same sinuous way, all of which gave rise to the name 'Style Métro' as a synonym for Art Nouveau.

Guimard's contemporary in Belgium, Victor Horta, was a cobbler's son who had originally studied music before moving to Paris to work in the studio of an architect and decorator Debuysson. Between 1892 and 1893, Horta designed a house for the engineer and geometry professor Emile Tassel, a house that would be the first movement towards the fully developed Art Nouveau style.

In the *Hôtel Tassel* (the word 'hotel' here means a significant residence or mansion, rather than a hostelry) a narrow, three-storey town house in a traditional terrace, Horta became one of the first architects to make extensive use of iron in a domestic building. He exploited its strength in supporting columns and its decorative capabilities in the free-flowing lines which are most apparent in the staircase. Here the supporting iron column is embellished with a capital of iron tendrils, the separate lines of which are repeated throughout the rest of the ironwork as well as in the paintwork, the mosaics and the colored glass panels.

The professor's office and laboratory were placed on the street front in a mezzanine floor (between the ground and first floor). In order to do this without excessively high or low ceilings, Horta changed the level of the ground-floor rooms in the rest of the house by raising them up half a storey. Cast-iron columns carry the weight of the building through the center of the house and, combined with

light wells, provide an open structure which is remarkably well lit for such a narrow building. The exterior of the *Hôtel Tassel* appears at first sight to be less remarkable than the interiors. Here however, Horta also used iron in columns and in an exposed beam between the first and second floor – something that had never been done in a private dwelling. The shallow curve of the bow window, though really only hinting at what is contained behind, harmonizes the *Hôtel Tassel's* façade with the existing, neighboring architecture.

Over the next ten years, Horta continued to explore the potentials of both iron and stone in a number of other houses in Brussels. His own house, the *Hôtel Horta*, shows again his treatment of these materials: on the balcony, iron supports curl like flowers while supporting pillars leaf out in a manner akin to the earlier staircase. The *Hôtel Solvay* is on a much more magnificent scale. Built for a wealthy client, Armand Solvay, the building uses the same spindles of iron as supports and decoration. The façade of the *Hôtel Solvay* is made up of an arrangement of flat and curved surfaces, out of which the ornament seems to grow. The *Hôtel van Eetvelde* was again an extravagant and spectacular house designed for a wealthy client (in this case a Baron)

with exotic tastes. In the *Hôtel van Eetvelde*, the central living space and communication place for the rest of the house is topped by a glazed dome supported by steel stanchions and decorated with stained glass.

Between 1896 and 1899 Horta produced his most original work, though it was completely different in function and design from his previous projects. The *Maison du Peuple* in Brussels, (now demolished) was built as the headquarters of the Belgian Socialist Party. For this building, there were several requirements that Horta had to meet: two large public spaces were needed for daily meetings and rallies, and a large auditorium with seating for two thousand for party conventions and staged presentations. Much of the front of the *Maison du Peuple* was to contain income-producing shops, offices and some smaller meeting rooms. On the façade, the iron frame of the building was visible, mixed with brick, stone and glass, and the Art Nouveau details were apparent in the ironwork balustrades and the stone carvings across the curving front of the building.

Inside, the auditorium was one of the classic statements of Art Nouveau, in which decoration was combined with the curvilinear struc-

LEFT: *The famous staircase from the* Hôtel Tassel. *The iron tendrils of the capitol are repeated in painted and mosaic decoration.*

RIGHT: *The façade of the* Hôtel Horta *explores the potential of both iron and stone.*

BELOW: *Art Nouveau door furniture on the* Hôtel Horta, *now a museum.*

BOTTOM: *Stained glass windows from the* Hôtel Van Eetvelde.

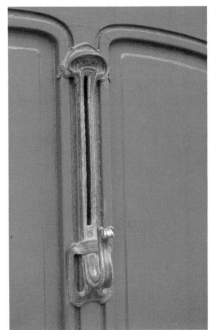

ture. The roof was carried on exposed curving steel girders, providing a lightweight yet rigid construction. Steel supports did away with the need for supporting columns (which usually restricted the views from the galleries); and over these supports, iron decorations climbed and twisted.

Horta's style grew out of the campaigns by architects in Belgium in the 1870s to develop a new, modern national style that was truthful and free from foreign influences. Such interests on the part of architects ran parallel with a general preoccupation with national identity that was aided by an accumulation of industrial wealth and by the political independence of Belgium.

In fact, the situation in Brussels at the end of the nineteenth century was in many respects similar to that in Barcelona, where in the 1860s a comparable Catalan revival had taken place when Madrid assumed sovereignty over the province, forbidding the use of the Catalan dialect. At first the revival was confined to social and political reforms, but it later took the form of a growing demand for Catalan independence. Despite support from the Church, Catalan independence was never granted and the claim would later emerge as a powerful factor in the Spanish Civil War.

The French architectural theorist Viollet-le-Duc, who advocated a return to regional building (and who had a pronounced effect on Horta and Guimard), was to be a major influence on the Catalan architect Antonio Gaudí (1852-1926). In his efforts to revive national architecture and in his desire to create new forms of expression, Gaudí was not alone, but he was unique in his mastery of the fantastic in an idiosyncratic organic style analogous to Art Nouveau.

An early project by Gaudí, the *Casa Vicens* (1878-1880) shows a marked 'Mudejar' influence: a combination of elements from Christian art and Arab ornamentation, which was at the time undergoing a fashionable revival in Spain. The *Casa Vicens* was built for a wealthy tile manufacturer, Manuel Vicens, who no doubt had some influence on the appearance of the building: the exteriors are of unplastered brick and ceramic tiles. (It must be noted however that Gaudí himself came from a family of potters.) During the course of construction, Gaudí would alter parts of the building until he was perfectly satisfied, often demolishing parts that he felt were unsuitable. *Casa Vicens* reveals Gaudí's characteristic sense of composition, which was combined with a truth to fine materials. Brick, stone and ceramic are blended together, rising to culminate in pinnacles which are both part of the overall composition and functional chimney crowns. Gaudí's feeling for nature is revealed in the floral motifs used in the ceramics and in the treatment of the palm motif in the wrought- and cast-iron gates. Inside, the oriental style reaches its apogée in the *fumoir* or smokers' lounge, a small room with a vaulted ceiling in a honeycomb pattern, lit by a cluster of Moorish lamps.

In 1882 Gaudí did his first work for the textile manufacturer Count Eusebi Guëll, who was to become a close and constant friend and patron. The first commission was for a porters' lodge, gate and stable

building for Guëll's property *Les Corts* in the suburbs of Barcelona. A year earlier in the *Ensanche*, the new town of Barcelona, plans were being made for the construction of a large church, *El Temple de la Sagrada Familia*, to be supported entirely by public contributions. The corner stone of the church was laid in 1882 and, after changes in architects, the commission was awarded to Gaudí in November 1883; he would continue work on the church until his death some forty-three years later.

While he was working on the *Sagrada Familia*, Gaudí began work on a new city home for Guëll in the Carrier Nau in 1885. Besides being the city residence of the Guëll family, the *Palacio Guëll* was also a sort of museum, exhibiting the family's antique collection and providing a background for the social life and activities organized there. For the façade itself Gaudí made twenty-five studies, finally submitting two to his patron. Guëll evidently chose the one plan Gaudí himself preferred, a plan which recalls the Venetian Gothic palaces. The palace is supported at basement level by columns. There are few walls at this level, to allow for maximum ventilation, which was necessary since Guëll's horses were to be stabled here. Columns are found throughout the palace; they range from heavy brick pillars in the basement to extremely fine columns inspired by the Alhambra Palace at Granada. Art Nouveau details appear in the ironwork and stonework in the bedroom and entrance gates. Some of the ironwork shows careful observation of floral motifs: the influence of William Morris and the Pre-Raphaelites was provided by Count Guëll's library, rich in English publications collected during his visits to England to study textile manufacturing techniques. Gaudí's interest in natural forms for both their decorative and structural possibilities is evident in his use of parabolic arches on the entrance gate, a motif

LEFT: *This building in the Guëll Park complex, by Antonio Gaudí, shows the blend of brick, stone and ceramic that makes his architecture unique.*

RIGHT: *Abstractedly sculpted ventilators covered in glazed ceramic, marble and crystal on the roof of the* Casa Mila.

repeated in the loggias, windows and in the parabolic dome covering the central courtyard. Providing a foretaste of the roofs of the *Casa Battló* and the *Casa Mila* is a complex arrangement of abstractedly sculpted ventilators covered in glazed ceramics, marble and crystal.

While work continued on the *Sagrada Familia* between 1900 and 1910, Gaudí gave up all reference to historical styles and built some of his most important works in the various forms suggested by Art Nouveau: Guëll Park, *Casa Mila* and *Casa Battló*.

In the *Casa Battló* (1904-1906) popularly known as the 'house of bones,' the problem was not constructing a new house but adapting an existing building, the basic structure of which was to be retained. The aim of the alterations was to change the original appearance of the façade and rear portion of the house and to adapt the main floor into living quarters for the owner, José Battlò Casanovas, who had decided to place his textile firm in the Paseo de Gracia, the most elegant part of the city. The lower part of the façade indeed resembles stripped bones, while the balconies look remarkably like vertebrae.

Inside, light is captured in the staircase wells by ceramic placques, some flat, others modelled in relief. In the staircase courtyard the light, mingling with blue glazed tiles, enters through a series of window openings and glass floors and penetrates the basement. Throughout the building there is fine woodwork: doors and their frames are carved, linking rooms together rather than dividing them. A carved oak staircase literally swirls up to the main floor where the best of Gaudí's interior work could be found, and for which Gaudí designed a complete suite of oak furniture including the famous curved-back sofas for two or three people.

The attic and terrace were built as a new floor for the old house, and here Gaudí applied his theory of roofing. He believed that buildings should have double roofs, in the same way that people should wear hats and carry sunshades. The roofs were to be built over a structure of brick arches that were distinct from the rest of the house, allowing for the changes in temperature to be absorbed. Thus, the 'sunshade' of the outer roof on the *Casa Battló* appears like a dragon's back, and its surface (like a dragon's scales) is faced in ceramic tiles. On the flat areas of the roof, Gaudí placed the chimneys which were decorated with glass fragments.

The continuing patronage of Eusebi Guëll led Gaudí to work on the Guëll Park in 1903. The Guëll family had acquired a large area of land on the outskirts of Barcelona at the end of the century. Among the property acquired was the Mas Montaner, an area facing southeast on a concave slope. From the top it is possible to see over the city to the Mediterranean. Guëll chose the site for an urban colony, following the pattern of English garden cities of the nineteenth century.

Within three years the basic constructions of the park were completed: the walls, gatehouses, main stairway and viaduct. The high wall on the main façade enclosing the precinct served the purpose of giving the inhabitants a sense of security and protection since at the beginning of the century the area was rather remote and isolated. A range of communal services was planned, including drinking water, lighting and power as well as pedestrian and vehicular routes. Other facilities were built around a large square, the lower part of which was for a market and the upper part for a 'theater of nature,' a recreational and cultural center. The square itself provided a rainwater collection surface which filled a large cistern placed under the porticoes of the market. In spite of the advantages of the new urban environment, the project failed financially, for only two dwelling plots were sold, one of them to Gaudí himself.

ABOVE LEFT: *The 'dragon's back' roof of the* Casa Battló *is made of two sections: an inner roof of parabolic arches and the outer tiled roof. This use of these arches allowed Gaudí to vary the line of the outer roof and regulated temperature changes within.*

ABOVE RIGHT: *One of the towers of the* Sagrada Familia *church in Barcelona. Four of a planned 13 towers were built. Their walls are pierced by openings which act like louvers to deflect rain.*

LEFT: *This bench at Guëll Park is built in prefabricated sections of plastered domes and sheathed in abstract patterns made of ceramics, glass and bottles.*

RIGHT: *The façade of the Nativity portal of the* Sagrada Familia.

LEFT: *Gaudí's treatment of the lower storeys of the Casa Battló has earned it the nickname 'House of Bones.'*

BELOW: *The Nativity portal and the four towers of the Sagrada Familia remained unfinished at the time of Gaudí's death, and are still under construction today.*

RIGHT: *Detail of balcony and iron decoration on the* Casa Vicens.

During the construction of the Guëll Park, Gaudí became an artist in the widest sense of the term. He constructed, sculpted and painted and broke up flat surfaces into different shapes. In the second stage of building, from 1907 to 1912, the long undulating bench was built; its movement was provided by prefabricated sections formed into plastered domes and sheathed in tiles. The abstracted 'collages' of ceramics, glass and bottles were some ten years in advance of abstract and Surrealist painting, but Gaudí had already employed the prefabricated building procedure during the first phase of construction in some parts of the stairway and the lower part of the colonnade.

Possibly Gaudí's major achievement and his most notable secular work is the *Casa Mila*, which dates from 1905 to 1910. It was his last residential work and perhaps his most ambitious. But like many of Gaudí's undertakings, the *Casa Mila* remains unfinished, lacking the monumental statue of the *Virgin and Child between Two Angels* that was intended to crown the structure. From the air it is possible to see the organization of the architecture: the two large inner courtyards and the curving movement of the façade. In the *Casa Mila*, Gaudí anticipated functionalism, doing away with the traditional concept of a block of apartments and giving rise to a new type of residence. For the first time in a Barcelona house, a ramp was planned to lead from the basement to the flat roof. But work stopped at the second floor and the ramp was removed. In its place a spiral staircase was fitted which wound around the inside walls of the courtyard to reach the living quarters. The whole house is held up by stone and brick columns with trelliswork replacing the supporting walls. Moveable

LEFT: *The roof of* Casa Mila *with its 'helmet headed' ventilators. The bannisters are a recent addition – the steps are placed perilously close to the edge of the deep courtyard.*

RIGHT: *The Karlsplatz Station was designed by Otto Wagner in 1898 for the Vienna urban transport system. A respected architect, Wagner did not believe that the project was too utilitarian to be worthwhile. Although the building is still based on classical lines, the new style of decoration is beginning to reveal itself.*

partitions in the rooms allow the building to be adapted for any use.

The *Casa Mila* occupies a corner space in the Paseo de Gracia, the main promenade in the Ensanche, and in order to exploit the free plan of the building, Gaudí rounded off the angles of the building, so the façades follow a series of serpentine lines. In the rounded windows, irregular columns and in the ironwork of the balconies we again find the forms of nature. The roof also follows a serpentine line. This is not merely decorative, but is formed by the arched supporting structure; variations in the height of the parabolic arches in the attic cause the undulating line. Built in bricks 'edge on,' the arches give maximum rigidity with a minimum of thickness, which facilitated the conversion of the attics into further apartments in 1954. On the roof terrace of the *Casa Mila*, the same rhythmic lines are apparent. Ventilators are lined up like a helmeted army, while the steps placed close to the edge of the deep courtyard must have produced dizziness if not fear, for originally there were no bannisters.

After stopping work on the *Casa Mila*, Gaudí devoted himself solely to religious architecture, of which the best-known example is undoubtedly the *Sagrada Familia*. The parts of the Temple of the Holy Family built by Gaudí include the crypt, the apse and the Nativity façade. The towers reach up 340 feet (100 meters), and a dome, which would have brought the structure to over 500 feet (150 meters), was planned but never executed.

The four towers over the eastern portal (the Nativity portal) are perhaps the most striking elements; instantly recognizable as the work of Gaudí, they have become a landmark of the city of Barcelona. The four towers were the first and only ones to be built out of a planned total of thirteen. The walls of the towers are pierced by openings, the sides of which are laced together by horizontal masonry. These function rather like louvres, protecting the interior from rain and deflecting sound. The towers above the portal are unmarked by sculptural elements in contrast with the lower section of the portal where the stone façade is clad with several large sculptures cast from cement in which are embedded fragments of glass.

Like all Gaudí's projects, the *Sagrada Familia* changed as building progressed. Constantly applying new theories and methods to the building, Gaudí developed a column based on a tilted tree structure which freed him from the need for flying buttresses to support the walls. Despite all his foresight, however, Gaudí was not an architect in the twentieth-century sense of the word: he was essentially still a

craftsman whose decisions were made in the course of construction rather than in definite paper plans. Even though a true Art Nouveau style only became apparent in his work after 1900, Gaudí has been hailed as a pioneer of twentieth-century structure and a forerunner of Nervi and Le Corbusier. In his refusal to continue the historicism of the nineteenth century, his interest in functional aspects of building, in his bold experimentation and in his individualism, Gaudí was truly a part of the Art Nouveau movement.

The various designs of European Art Nouveau were exhibited for the first time at the Universal Exposition in Paris in 1900, followed by a second exhibition in Turin in 1902. From these, artists on the continent became more acquainted with the English movement. A further understanding in Germany and Austria of Mackintosh's work in particular was aided by Hermann Muthesias (1861-1927), the cultural attaché at the German embassy in London from 1896 to 1903. In 1901 Muthesias published his book *Die Englische Baukunst der Gegenwart* and from 1904 to 1908 produced three volumes of articles and letters, *Das Englische Haus* which praised the work of Mackintosh and Baillie Scott.

The German Art Nouveau, or *Jugendstil* designers, like their British, Belgian and French contemporaries, began their careers as painters and graphic artists and later turned to design and architecture under the influence of Ruskin, Morris and the Arts and Crafts Movement. The *Jugendstil* only truly manifested itself after 1897 and, from the beginning, was split between ornate curvilinear forms derived from nature such as those of Horta and Guimard, and more rectilinear abstract forms like those of Mackintosh.

By 1900 German design was gripped by Art Nouveau ornamentation. The Elvira Studio by August Endell (1871-1925), built in 1897 and destroyed in 1944, had certain affinities with the work of Guimard and Gaudí in its deliberately asymmetrical walls and openings and in the curving ironwork of the windows. But the motif, like a breaking

ABOVE: *Otto Wagner's design for an art gallery in Vienna.*

LEFT: *Otto Wagner's 1906 design for the* Friedenspalast *in the Hague.*

RIGHT: *The Steinhof Church (1906) in Vienna typifies Wagner's later style. Under the influence of Josef Olbrich, he moved further from classical architectural forms.*

RIGHT: *The Steinhof Church (1906) in Vienna typifies Wagner's later style. Under the influence of Josef Olbrich, he moved further from classical architectural forms.*

wave, which dominated the façade is unique. Through the avant-garde review *Pan*, the taste for the Art Nouveau spread throughout the German-speaking countries, but soon afterwards the influence of the Vienna School began to be seen.

In 1895 Otto Wagner (1841-1918) published his book *Moderne Architektur*, in which he stated that architecture should concentrate on 'modern life' instead of imitating past styles. Wagner's ideas bore fruit in the form of the *Vereinigung Bildender Kunstler Österreichs* (The Austrian Fine Art Association), a breakaway group of artists who adopted the name *Sezession* and published the journal *Ver Sacrum*. Their motto was 'Der Zeit ihre Kunst – der Kunst ihre Freiheit' (to the age its art – to art its freedom), a concept similar to that expressed in Wagner's book. While Wagner's early commissions for projects such as the construction of the stations of the *Stadtbahn*, the transport system, betray a certain classicism; a building which shows his integration of the new decorative influences from the rest of Europe is the Maiolica House, a block of apartments over shops in a suburb developed outside the Ringstrasse in Vienna. (In 1857 Emperor Franz Joseph II had ordered the demolition of the fortifications surrounding the old city and the construction in their place of the Ringstrasse to link the old city with the rapidly developing new suburbs.)

In overall form the Maiolica House is similar to many other basic-ally classical blocks in Vienna: the Art Nouveau influence is apparent in the treatment of the surface with colored maiolica tiles, with a sun-flower motif repeated on the balconies. Wagner's later style, as exemplified in the Steinhof Church (1906), came about through his contact with the experiments of younger architects, in particular Josef Olbrich (1869-1908), who worked in Wagner's studio from 1894 to 1898. Olbrich abandoned almost all conventional decoration and replaced it with plant and tree forms, using a wide variety of materials and a range of color effects. In the *Ernst Ludwig Haus* designed for Ernst Ludwig of Hesse and his archduchess in Darmstadt in 1901, the mosaic in gold which frames the entrance and the blue-green mosaics of the terraces are typical of Art Nouveau.

Joining Olbrich in the *Sezession* and in Wagner's office was Josef Hoffmann (1870-1955). Hoffmann and his colleague Kolomon Moser (1868-1918) had organized an exhibition in Vienna in 1901 in which they displayed a series of furnished rooms. Some of the rooms they designed themselves, others were the work of Ashbee and Mackintosh, but all were met with great approval by the Viennese public and much of the furniture on exhibition was sold. After visiting England and Ashbee, Hoffmann met with Mackintosh in Glasgow. On their return to Vienna, both Hoffmann and Moser decided to try and bridge the gap between artist and craftsman to provide good-quality unified

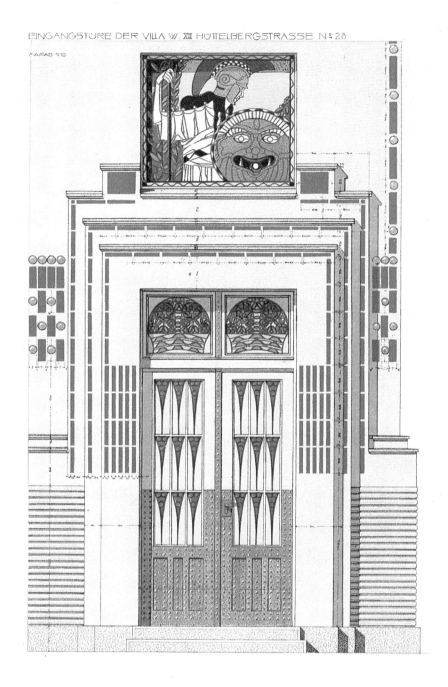

design. With Ruskin and Morris as their spiritual guides, they founded the *Wiener Werkstadt* in 1903 with financial backing from Fritz Warndofer, who had also been a patron of Mackintosh. The *Werkstätte* established the fashion in Vienna for clear lines and pure forms; they made few attempts to approach the needs of machine production, however, for the *Werkstadt* was still essentially a craft-based organization.

Overshadowing all of Hoffmann's commissions is his magnum

ABOVE LEFT: *Otto Wagner's design for a villa on the Ringstrasse shows the development of his style, particularly in comparison with the Karlsplatz station.*

ABOVE RIGHT: *The Vienna Secession Building (1897-98) by Josef Olbrich differs little in plan and general arrangement from the customary exhibition halls; in the treatment of the façade, however, Olbrich abandoned classical ornamentation in favor of tree forms.*

LEFT: *One of a pair of apartment blocks with shops below, Otto Wagner's* Maiolica House *has its façade clad in colored tiles with a weaving sunflower motif repeated in the balconies.*

RIGHT: *Peter Behrens' own house in the artists' colony at Darmstadt uses bands of green terracotta to create a rippling effect.*

opus, the *Palais Stoclet* in Brussels, designed in 1905. It was built for Belgian financier Adolphe Stoclet and his wife Suzanne on lines very similar to Mackintosh's plan for the 'Art Lover's House' for the competition organized by Koch, although it differs in the repetitive asymmetrical series of small windows. The volume of the *Palais Stoclet* is broken down into squares edged with dark bands; the main decorative feature of the exterior is the metal molding which frames the windows and lines the edges of the walls, which are themselves

ABOVE: *Built for a Belgian financier to house a collection of art works, the* Palais Stoclet *(1905) was undoubtedly Josef Hoffmann's masterpiece.*

LEFT: *In the interior of the* Palais Stoclet, *Hoffmann made great use of highly reflective surfaces of glass, marble and polished wood. Gustav Klimt's mosaics* Expectation *and* Fulfilment *complete the overall effect of glittering opulence.*

ABOVE: *In 1903 Hoffmann co-founded the* Wiener Werkstadt *with financial backing from Fritz Warndorfer. The* Werkstadt *established the fashion in Vienna for cleaner lines and purer forms, such as this stained limed oak hall clock by Hoffmann.*

RIGHT: *In the work of Auguste Perret, reinforced concrete first achieved architectural status. In this 1906 garage in the Rue Ponthieu, Paris, the material is stated on the outside as well as inside in a way that upset traditional ideas about architecture and engineering.*

covered with thin slabs of white Norwegian marble. Designed to show off the works of art collected by the Stoclets as well as to entertain the artistic and cultural élite of Europe, the *Palais Stoclet* makes use of regular geometric forms to create atmosphere and mood. There are rooms that are light and airy, making use of the highly reflective surfaces of glass, polished wood and marble, while others are dark, like the dining room which contains Klimt's mosaics *Expectations* and *Fulfilment*.

A founder member of the Munich *Sezession* in 1893 and later a member of Ernst Ludwig Hesse's Darmstadt colony of artists was Peter Behrens (1868-1940). Behrens' contribution to the 1901 ex-

hibition was his own house, the *Haus Behrens*. Bands of green terracotta tiles create a rippling effect against the edges of brickwork, but the curvilinear Art Nouveau is beginning to be straightened out, becoming more geometric. This approach shows the way in which Behrens' work was to develop in the following years. His main works before World War I were designed for AEG, a large German electrical company for which Behrens designed not only industrial buildings, but the company's products and publicity material. Behrens' outstanding architectural construction was the Turbine Factory, built in 1909. In this, the steel frame is evident, with wide glass panes replacing the walls. Heavy stonework is still employed, but it has been

softened at the corners. When it was built, the Turbine Factory was probably the largest shed in Berlin, for most factories at the time were lower, wider and had cast-iron columns supporting lightweight roofs which provided the lighting and ventilation. But Behrens' Turbine Factory was far from being a straightforward design in iron and glass like the nineteenth century railway sheds; it was a work of art, which some have called a 'temple to industry.'

Although the apartment block by Auguste Perret (1874-1954) at 25 bis rue Franklin of 1902 has decorative panels in an Art Nouveau leaf pattern which closely follow the contours of the framework, and its concrete posts and beams are clad in terracotta, the eight-storey block was the first domestic building to use a concrete skeleton. Inside, the load-bearing pillars allow the walls, now free of their structural role, to be arranged according to functional and spatial needs.

LEFT: *Peter Behrens' Turbine Hall for the AEG factory in Berlin was built in 1909. At the time it was possibly the largest shed in Berlin. The steel frame is still evident, but the hall was originally clad in stone with rounded edges.*

BELOW: *The decorative panels of Perret's 1902 apartments in the Rue Franklin, Paris, closely follow the contours of the frame of the building.*

France continued to produce artists and designers who worked in the Art Nouveau idiom long after the style had reached its peak in other countries such as Germany and America, where it was superseded by the Modern style. In the production of Art Nouveau furniture France had two centers: Paris and Nancy. And though each city fostered its own style, both worked on the principle of using nature and natural forms as a source of inspiration. The French cabinet makers used wood as if it were clay. Not confining decoration merely to flat surfaces, they would ignore the natural grain of wood and force it to obey their style, twisting it into fluid shapes that captured the hothouse exuberance of the 'Style 1900.'

It was the energy of Emile Gallé (1846-1904), a passionate botanist and a self-proclaimed Symbolist, who created the *Ecole de Nancy*. Gallé began this career as a ceramicist before venturing into glass, for which he is probably best known. Then, in 1885, he moved into furniture making. The Nancy School furniture has forms which tend to be heavier than their Parisian counterparts (where natural forms were more stylized, refined and even more elegant) and some of Gallé's furniture, like the fabulous Butterfly Bed were works of pure symbolism. Here, the head and footboards are in the form of giant butterflies, representing dawn and twilight, inlaid with mother of pearl and various toned woods. It is clear that there was no way that furniture like this could be produced cheaply: Gallé's ideal commission for designs such as these was to create all the furniture and objects d'art for a single room or house of a wealthy client.

LEFT: *This 1900 desk by Emile Gallé is one of several examples of the design known as 'La Forêt de Lorraine.'*

BELOW: *The head and footboards of Gallé's Butterfly Bed, representing dawn and dusk, typify his highly wrought Symbolism.*

FAR LEFT: *Fiercely proud of his native Lorraine, Gallé used local woods for his elaborate marquetry, despite the distinctly oriental feel of this 1900 firescreen.*

LEFT: *Louis Majorelle often modelled his pieces in clay before carving. In this firescreen, the carved motif of cow parsley is repeated in the embroidered inset panel.*

BELOW LEFT: *Following the commercial success of Majorelle and Gallé, a number of firms started producing furniture in the Art Nouveau style such as this Nancy School settee (c 1900).*

RIGHT: *Staircase by Louis Majorelle in carved wood with metal.*

A further characteristic of the Nancy School furniture was the sense of regional pride: local plants and woods were used in marquetry or in relief carving. These formed part of a repertoire of three hundred woods that Gallé used, exploiting each wood's own unique qualities and potential. Gallé's Firescreen (1900), exhibited at the Paris Exhibition of 1900, demonstrates his use of a rich variety of carved and inlaid woods. The screen itself is of carved ash, the applied design is of oak, zebra wood and sabicue, and the marquetry is of amboyna and walnut.

Louis Majorelle (1859-1926) was trained as a painter, but returned to Nancy in 1879 to take over his father's cabinet-making business. After coming under the influence of Gallé, Majorelle gave up making furniture in the Rococo style to work in naturalistic Art Nouveau forms. At the 1900 exhibition, he displayed a room whose theme was the water lily. Although he did use naturalistic carved and inlaid details, his designs were often more elegant than Gallé's. It was characteristic of the efforts required that Majorelle often modelled his pieces in clay before they were made of wood.

Eugène Vallin perhaps came closest to the heavy curving and molded forms that we saw in Guimard's Métro station entrances. Where English interiors normally consisted of separate pieces which harmonized, Vallin's furniture was designed from the outset as an integral part of a homogenous room. This approach, coupled with Vallin's tendency to choose dark woods, tended to result in a very formal and often forbidding impression; one feels that one is intruding on the room itself.

Alexandre Charpentier (1856-1909), a sculptor who later became a decorator, was part of the Parisian group *Les Cinq* which was at the center of the crafts revival in Paris. Charpentier took the Art Nouveau curve to its extreme, an approach that is particularly evident in the Rotating Music Stand, the base of which is more like melting wax than wood. Like many designers of the Art Nouveau period, Gallé, Majorelle and Charpentier did not confine themselves to designing and producing furniture. Given the Art Nouveau insistence on the unity of the arts, it is not surprising that the figures we associate with architecture, such as Guimard, Gaudí, Mackintosh and van de Velde, should have designed furniture, or that those we associate with furniture should have designed glass, silver and jewelry.

BELOW LEFT: *Much of Eugène Vallin's furniture such as this sellette (c 1900) was designed to be featured in a particular room. His frequent choice of dark woods tend to give his rooms a somewhat somber appearance.*

BELOW RIGHT: *Alexandre Charpentier began his career as a sculptor. Often ignoring the natural grain of the wood, Charpentier took the Art Nouveau curve to its extreme in furniture such as this music stand (1901).*

RIGHT: *Display cabinet (c 1900) with a marquetry design of plants, berries and flowers, possibly by Majorelle. On the shelves are a Bohemeian vase in iridiscent glass and silver, decanter and glasses of c 1900 and a bowl and cover made by Wurttembergische Metallwarenfabrik.*

FAR RIGHT: *This dining room furnished by Eugène Vallin is a fine example of Nancy School furniture in its Art Nouveau setting.*

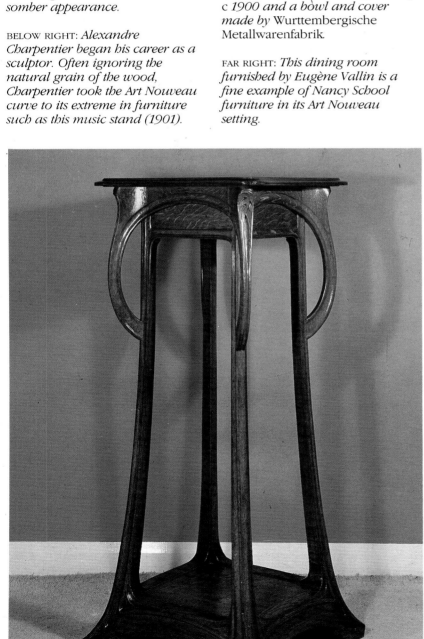

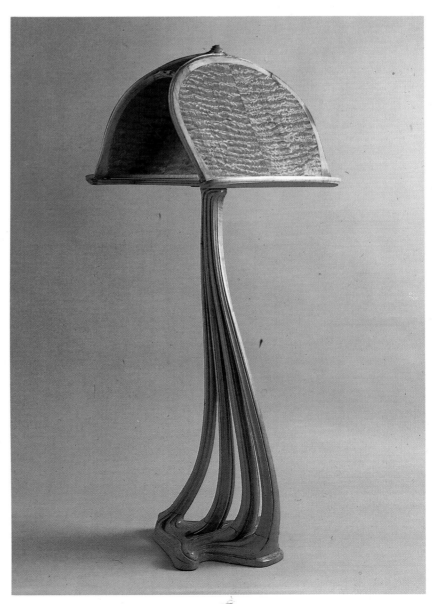

LEFT: *Hector Guimard did not confine his talents to Métro station entrances but translated his curls and slender forms into furniture. Compared with the furniture of the Nancy School, Parisian pieces seem more elegant.*

RIGHT: *Music Cabinet (1900), by Alexandre Charpentier.*

RIGHT: *This dining table and set of nine chairs were designed by Henri van de Velde for the Bloemenwerf House in Uccle, Belgium in 1895.*

BELOW: *This oak dining chair is one of a set designed by Charles Rennie Mackintosh for Miss Cranston's Argyle Street Tea Rooms in Glasgow, although they may never have been used there as they remained in the possession of the Mackintoshes for several years.*

BELOW RIGHT: *Tiffany Studios side chair (1911). Art Institute of Chicago, gift of Mrs Philip Wrigley. Although Tiffany's is a name more usually associated with glassware, the workshops produced a wide range of products.*

RIGHT: *Henri van de Velde designed this walnut sidechair for the dining room of his own house in Uccle.*

RIGHT: *This four-fold screen by Alphonse Mucha is decorated with panels depicting* Les Temps du Jour. *Mucha, like many other artists of this period, successfully crossed the boundaries from one art form to another.*

BELOW: *Austrian Art Nouveau furniture. From left: chair by Thonet (c 1905); cabinet by Koloman Moser (c 1903); three-fold screen by Josef Hoffmann (c 1899); square-shaped chair by Koloman Moser (c 1903).*

LEFT: *The bar in the Auditorium Building. Sullivan was largely responsible for the decoration and ornamentation of the building.*

ABOVE: *Interior of the Chicago Auditorium by Dakmar Adler and Louis Sullivan (1886).*

As in Europe, architects and designers in America were moving away from the traditional historical styles of nineteenth-century architecture. For most American designers, the styles and motifs of the Gothic or the Renaissance were reminders of the past, hangovers from the years of colonization that were inappropriate for a new country. For many Americans, European architecture came to symbolize the dependence of America on Europe for its culture. It was in Chicago, the growing, thriving commercial center, that the new approaches to architecture would be developed. H H Richardson's (1838-1886) neo-Romanesque Marshall Field Wholesale Store, begun in 1885 and completed in 1887, a year after his death, marks the point of departure for the developments of Chicago architect Louis Sullivan (1856-1924). Sullivan, who was born in Boston, the son of an Irish dancing master, spent a year studying architecture at the Massachusetts Institute of Technology in 1872 and a further year in Paris in 1874 at the École des Beaux Arts in the studio of J A E Vaudremer. By 1875 Sullivan was in Chicago and in 1881 he entered into partnership with Dakmar Adler, a partnership that would last until 1895.

During the early years of their partnership, Adler and Sullivan were concerned with the urgent needs of a booming Chicago, which was then in the process of being rebuilt after its destruction by fire in 1871. The development of fireproof steel-frame building techniques, with their ability to provide multistorey buildings, allowed property speculators to develop sites in downtown Chicago to their optimum. And once the elevator had been perfected, the height of buildings with steel frames could be doubled again.

LEFT: *Details of the ornament surrounding windows of Sullivan's Wainwright Building, St Louis (1890).*

Adler and Sullivan's early commissions were, on the whole, for small office structures, warehouses and department stores. limited to around six storeys. But all this altered when, in 1886, they were commissioned to design the Auditorium Building in Chicago. The brief was to plan, on a half-block site, a large modern opera house flanked on two sides by eleven storeys of private dwellings, offices and a hotel. In the auditorium Adler allowed for a variety of audiences (2500 for concerts and 1000 for conventions) to be housed comfortably by using folding ceiling panels and vertical screens, while the acoustic requirements determined the nature and extent of the decorative forms: a series of concentric eliptical arches allow the sound to be carried from the proscenium-arched stage upward and outward into the back of the auditorium.

Externally, Sullivan varied the facing material of the auditorium building, emphasizing the verticality of the building by using rusticated granite blocks on the lower three floors and smooth sandstone from the fourth floor upward. While there is little decoration, the colonnade of the hotel verandah on the lake front betrays a hint of orientalism. Sullivan, like many of his contemporary architects, was to use decoration not simply to embellish a building but also to emphasize its structural elements. The Wainwright Building in St Louis (1890-91) was Sullivan's first attempt to apply his compositional principles to a high-rise frame building. The essential feature of a skyscraper is the fact that it has numerous identical floors. Apart from the

ABOVE: *Decorative terracotta block from the Felsenthal Store (1905), 701-709 47th St, Chicago by Louis Sullivan. (84.5×85×20cm)*

LEFT: *The National Farmers' Bank, Owatonna, Minnesota (1907-08) by Louis Sullivan.*

ground and first floors and the top floor, the intermediate levels could not be differentiated without considerably altering the structure. Sullivan had the idea of treating the whole of the middle area as one element by emphasizing the vertical partitions and contrasting them with the horizontal lowest sections and the crowning Art Nouveau attic. The horizontal spandrels upon which each storey is placed are recessed to allow the vertical piers to flow upward uninterrupted.

In the Guaranty Building, Buffalo (1895), Sullivan perfected the design he had been developing: a three-layer building, with the first layer of ground and mezzanine floors, the second layer with ten floors of offices, and the third layer consisting of a decorated attic storey and flat roof. Verticality is again the overriding quality of the building, a quality which is emphasized by mullions which run uninterrupted from the mezzanine level to the roof. Ornamental terracotta is worked in a filigree style and the motifs used are repeated in the ornate metalworks in the lobby. Only the ground-floor plate-glass windows and marble-clad walls are left free of ornament.

Sullivan was a prolific designer of architectural decoration, and produced many different kinds for a variety of purposes. Two years after Horta began his *Maison du Peuple*, Sullivan began work on the Schlessinger-Meyer Department Store (now Carson Pirie Scott and Co) in which he specified that the windows, to allow in extra light, should be larger and longer than those normally found in public buildings. These windows – much copied by designers of other buildings – came to be called 'Chicago Windows.' The enlarging of the windows to allow extra light on the sales floors demonstrates how Sullivan followed his dictum that 'form follows function.' Although the upper-storey windows are starkly functional, those of the first two floors are surrounded by decorative ironwork, composed of swirling scrolls, leaves and flowers. The profusion of Art Nouveau decoration, however, does not hide the exposed structural grid of the steel-cage construction. In this project, located at what has been called 'the world's busiest corner,' Sullivan demonstrated that the work of engineers could be put to architectural use, meeting the physical as well as the emotional and aesthetic needs of people.

After work on the Carson Pirie Scott building was completed in 1903, Sullivan's career declined and he received few important commissions. From then on he devoted much of his time to writing, although he was commissioned to produce five small-town banks, in which he concentrated on decoration. His writings bore fruit in 1924, the year he died, when Sullivan completed his books *Autobiography of an Idea* and *A System of Architectural Ornament According With A Philosophy of Man's Power.*

ABOVE: *Detail of the façade of the Chicago Auditorium.*

BELOW: *Ornamental ironwork around the windows of the Carson Pirie Scott and Co store.*

RIGHT: *The Carson, Pirie Scott and Co department store in Chicago by Louis Sullivan.*

LEFT: *Perspective drawing by Frank Lloyd Wright of the Ward Willet House, Highlands Park, Illinois, (1902).*

BELOW: *The Ward Willet House. Although he never publicly acknowledged its influence, Japanese architecture played an important role in Wright's designs.*

It was Frank Lloyd Wright (1865-1959) who would surpass Sullivan in his work and in his influence on other architects. Wright was 18 when he joined the studio of Adler and Sullivan in 1887, when they were working on the Chicago Auditorium. While assisting on this project, Wright also began working on his own, opening his own studio in 1893. But Wright's career as an architect really began in 1889, when he built his own house in Oak Park, Illinois. Here he developed an organic approach to structure in which the exterior and interior would reflect their interrelationship and every detail (like the furniture) was individually designed to fit, often built-in to delimit the interior space.

Wright was brought up on the nineteenth-century textbooks of Viollet-le-Duc and Owen Jones, whose *Grammar of Ornament* he owned. The taste for floral ornament that Jones advocated in his book (in which over half of the ornamental examples were Eastern or Celtic in origin) was no doubt reinforced by Sullivan's designs, for some of Wright's earlier decorative and ornamental details were derived from the plant forms beloved of the Art Nouveau era.

Another influence on Wright's development was that of oriental art and architecture, an interest sparked off by the Japanese Pavilion at the World's Columbian Exposition in Chicago in 1893. Wright became an avid collector of Japanese prints, decorative screens and oriental ceramics. The Japanese houses, with their simple structure, decorative use of structural devices and the flexible organization of interior space, all placed in a close relationship with the natural environment, were to be an influence, albeit one that Wright would never personally acknowledge.

In addition, many of Wright's earliest principles of architecture and decoration were developed from the line of nineteenth-century thinkers that culminated in the Arts and Crafts Movement: in 1897 Wright himself had been a founding member of the Chicago Arts and Crafts society, founded at social reformer Jane Addams' Hull House and modelled on London's Toynbee Hall. In Wright's own house at Oak Park, the inglenook represents the spirit of the Arts and Crafts aesthetic, complete with the motto 'Truth is Life' carved on the chimney-breast above mantle.

By 1900 Wright was familiar with the published work of Mackintosh, van de Velde, Berlage, Loos and Wagner. By 1904 he had the opportunity to admire Olbrich's interiors exhibited that year at the Louisiana Purchase Exhibition.

Wright's homes have been said to begin with the hearth as the central point and to grow outward. This plan had already been incorporated into vernacular building in America, where rooms were clustered around the heat source. A further characteristic of American vernacular building is the porch, used both as a shelter and as an outdoor living space. Both these elements are to be found in Wright's work, where the porch often becomes a cantilevered roof or coach gate (*porte-cochère*), the forerunner of today's car-port.

The first period of Wright's work – up to 1910 – includes numerous one-family houses in the rectilinear style of Art Nouveau, the so-called Prairie Houses, the Unity Temple at Oak Park (which was his first concrete building) and an office block, the *Larkin Building* in Buffalo, which was one of the first air-conditioned office buildings. Wright's goal, like that of many of his European contemporaries, was to achieve an environment that would embrace and affect the whole of society. With this intention, the main entrance to the Larkin Building is adorned with a cascade of water falling from a symbolic relief, on which the inscription reads 'Honest labor needs no master, simple justice needs no slaves.' The relief was created by sculptor Richard Bock, whose work, in its symbolism, was close to the European *Sezession* style.

Wright's architectural program for the Prairie Houses included reducing the number of necessary parts of the house and keeping separate rooms to a minimum, allowing light and air to permeate the whole building. He also wanted to eliminate rooms as 'boxes,' with the whole house as one 'box,' by making the walls into screens and the proportions more on a human scale. He wanted to eliminate combinations of building materials in favor of a single material as far as possible, with ornament that grew naturally out of this material.

BELOW: *In the early part of his career, Frank Lloyd Wright designed many one-family houses in the rectilinear mode of Art Nouveau, such as the Winslow House in River Forest, Illinois (1893).*

LEFT: *Many of Wright's houses, such as the Thomas House at Oak Park, Illinois (1901), are said to have begun at the central hearth and grown outward. This practice of grouping rooms around the main heating source was already established in vernacular building in America.*

BELOW: *Vernacular American buildings often included a porch; at the Robie House, Wright developed this feature into a cantilevered roof. As far as possible, Wright avoided combinations of materials in favor of a single material out of which the ornamentation grew.*

Since Wright believed that geometric forms and straight lines were the natural forms and lines of the machines that were used in building, the interiors of his buildings took on the same characteristic straight lines. Furthermore, the furnishings were to be 'one' with the building, designed in simple terms for machine production. The furniture Wright designed for his own home included chairs with tall spindle backs; later chairs would use slats or a single sloping board in the back.

Yet Wright believed his buildings to be characterized in their details by Sullivan's idiom: some of Wright's most beautiful ornament is Sullivanesque. Decorative friezes of stylized oak trees, flowers and foliage contained in rectangles and circles appear in many of his houses. In his own house there is a jigsawed ceiling grille behind which were placed recessed lamps. The grille's design combines patterns of oak leaves and geometric elements, an echo of the medieval stained glass and Celtic interlaces that influenced the Scottish Art Nouveau designers.

Until 1909, when Wright went to Europe, he held a considerable influence over both his contemporary designers in America and his clients. In some cases this influence extended beyond the design of the house to the design of every single item within it, and, in some cases such as the Martin House of 1906 Wright even decided on the choice and arrangement of his client's Japanese prints and ceramics.

His larger buildings of Wright's early period share the same characteristic spatial concepts as his smaller houses. The Unity Chapel (1906) has its space articulated in all directions: the ceiling grid, balconies and open staircase all contribute. Where in the houses Wright had used a horizontal band such as a frieze which ran

ABOVE: *As much light as possible was allowed to permeate the interiors of Wright's buildings. The Arthur Heurtley House in Oak Park, Illinois (1902) has windows running the length of the building and inside walls that are turned into screens to allow the passage of light into the interiors.*

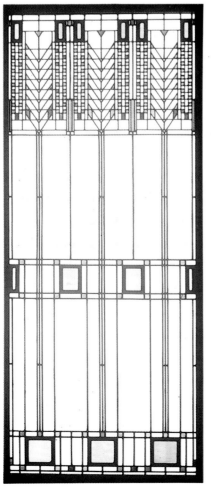

LEFT: *The rectilinear style of Art Nouveau was continued throughout Wright's interiors, in decorative glass such as this* Tree of Life *design, and in the furniture.*

RIGHT: *Oak high back spindle chair (c 1908), by Frank Lloyd Wright.*

along the top edge of the doors to link each opening to the next, he now used these lines more subtly, to establish the relationship between planes and spaces. Each line makes us aware of the depth and solidity of the form as well as the size of the open spaces. The pattern that is made by the lines and their dark appearance against light walls are like those used by Mackintosh, or by Hoffmann on the exterior of the *Palais Stoclet*.

Up until the Depression, Wright continued to produce designs for silver, ceramics, glass and furniture, as well as the covers for *Liberty Magazine*. His *Autobiography* (1932) appeared at a time when his career was at a standstill, before it enjoyed a revival in 1936 with the house Fallingwater. Much of Wright's later work shows a continuity with his earlier designs, even to the point of retaining something of the Arts and Crafts atmosphere.

The impact of the Arts and Crafts movement in the United States was also felt by the Greene Brothers. Charles Sumner Greene (1868-1957) and his brother Henry Mather Greene (1870-1954) were born in Ohio, and later moved to St Louis. The Greenes studied at the Manual Training High School (set up by a family friend, Calvin Milton Woodward), in the hope of following in their great-grandfather's footsteps by becoming architects.

Under Woodward's guidance, the Greenes became influenced by Ruskin and Morris, learning the skills of craftsmanship and the relationship between form, function and materials. After studying architecture at MIT, each joined a distinguished architect's firm in Boston. In 1893 the brothers left the East Coast: their careers there had not developed as they had anticipated, and they decided to visit their parents who had moved to Pasadena, California. En route, the brothers also visited the Japanese Pavilion at the World's Columbian Exhibition. This, and their first real commission (to design a house for a butcher), led the brothers to establish a practice in California. Over the next two decades, Greene and Greene would design 180 buildings, 70 of which survive today.

The Kinney Kendall Building in Pasadena (1896), designed two years after the brothers had set up their practice, was one of the firm's few commercial structures. The Greenes, like their avant-garde American contemporaries, departed from European historicism, replacing it with strong, clear lines. By 1900 they had completely abandoned all the popular historical styles.

ABOVE LEFT: *The Unity Chapel in Oak Park, Illinois (1906) was Frank Lloyd Wright's first building in concrete.*

BELOW LEFT: *Inside the Unity Chapel, patterns of dark lines against light walls mark the depth of areas and enclose open space.*

RIGHT: *This oak side chair was designed by Frank Lloyd Wright in 1904 (102.2×40.5×46.4cm).*

BELOW: *Wright's Barnsdale House, Los Angeles (1917-22) was also known as the Hollyhock House on account of the stylized plant forms that were beginning to appear in Wright's work.*

ABOVE: *The Gamble House, Pasadena (1896) by Greene and Greene is possibly their best known work, and became the center for the Arts and Crafts movement on the West Coast.*

LEFT: *The interior of the Gamble House, showing the hearth and built-in bench.*

RIGHT: *The dining room of the Gamble House.*

The Gamble House in Pasadena (1908), which became a center for the Arts and Crafts movement on the West Coast and possibly the Greenes' best known work, made use of a low overhanging roof and sleeping porches, giving an open quality appropriate to the lifestyle and climate of Southern California. Its interiors rival Mackintosh's library at the Glasgow School of Art. The Greenes' success, however, rested on their ability to give a quality of design to the most modest of small, two-storey houses.

Following Charles's honeymoon in England and Italy in 1901, the Greenes produced their first house in the true Arts and Crafts mode. The house was fitted with furniture made by Gustav Stickley (1857-1946), whose workshops, called the United Crafts, were organized on a guild basis under the influence of Ruskin and Morris. Stickley had also visited Bing's shop 'L'Art Nouveau' in Paris in 1898 and brought back with him furniture, glass, jewelry, textiles and metalwork in the new style. In the same year he had visited England, studying the works of Mackmurdo, Ashbee and Baillie Scott. On his return, Stickley set out to produce furniture in the Art Nouveau style (with the Japanese and medieval elements clearly stated), but his cabinet-making attitude led him to produce straight-lined, hand-finished and somewhat heavy furniture. A few pieces have inlaid decoration, but on the whole Stickley believed that all ornamentation should be functional. Each piece of 'Craftsman' furniture was marked with Stickley's motto *'Als Ik Kan'* (As I Can) after Morris's *'Si je puis.'*

Charles and Henry Greene's partnership was the perfect collaboration: they both had had the same manual training and shared a common philosophy and, while Charles would produce the more sinuous and naturalistic forms of Art Nouveau, Henry used the more rectilinear mode; the combination of these approaches brought a sense of unity to their work.

ABOVE LEFT: *Greene and Greene modeled this leaded glass light on Japanese sword guards.*

ABOVE RIGHT: *The flamboyance of Charles Rohlfs' furniture rivaled that of the French.*

BELOW: *American taste in furniture preferred simple craftsmanship that reflected the country's own traditions and values. This oak stool (34×50.9×35.5cm) by Leopold and George Stickley is akin to Arts and Crafts pieces.*

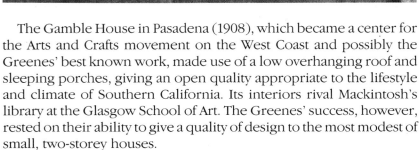

The influence of the Japanese Pavilion would remain with the Greenes. The Tichenor House at Long Beach, California (1904) gave the brothers their chance to explore and develop the possibilities of oriental forms, and the opportunity to turn functional forms into decorative elements. Even the light fixtures of leaded stained glass used a medallion form derived from Japanese *tsubas*, or sword guards.

Though the Greenes' work was often praised in journals of the day and the brothers received visits from their European admirers, by 1915 their partnership was slowly petering out. While Henry continued to practice as an architect, Charles became increasingly influenced by the oriental, in particular by Buddhism. The partnership of Greene and Greene was finally dissolved in 1922.

American Art Nouveau furniture was mostly mass produced, whereas in France the best Art Nouveau pieces, such as those of the Nancy School, were hand made, each of them unique. Since the structural forms of the curvilinear Art Nouveau did not lend themselves easily to machine production, the American designers standardized the motifs used in European Art Nouveau: the tulips, lilies and women with flowing hair. Thus in American furniture, Art Nouveau was largely confined to ornament.

One American designer who did fully use the curvilinear Art Nouveau style and created individually crafted pieces was Charles Rohlfs (1853-1936). In the early stages of his career, Rohlfs confined himself to simple, functional but high-quality pieces, decorated in a style akin to Sullivan's ornament. By 1898 Rohlfs was creating Art Nouveau furniture that was closer to the European styles than any other furniture being produced in America. On the whole, however, the curving, flowing lines of European Art Nouveau could not really compete with America's end-of-the-century passion for its own history and its search for its own national identity.

BELOW: *Hall bench designed by Greene and Greene for the Blacker House, Pasadena (c 1907).*

RIGHT: *Inlaid Honduras mahogany armchair designed by Greene and Greene for the Blacker House (c 1907).*

Just as Art Nouveau did not miraculously appear from nowhere, the style did not suddenly vanish, but grew with the technical changes of the age and altered its forms to suit the times. It is useful to remember that many of the leading figures of Art Nouveau died only recently. Throughout the twentieth century both the rectilinear forms that had been favored by the Scottish and Viennese and the curvilinear forms of Art Nouveau were to reappear. Furthermore, the Art Nouveau designers' interest in the function of objects, and their investigations into the capabilities of materials, were continued by twentieth-century practitioners.

The idea that Art Nouveau suddenly disappeared on the eve of World War I is a fiction that has been adopted for the sake of neatness, part of the general tendency on the part of historians to place movements or styles into convenient time slots. But Erich Mendelsohn's use of organic curvilinear forms in the Potsdam Tower (1920) shows how misleading this attitude can be. Though now destroyed, Mendelsohn's drawings show that he was aiming for a plasticity of form that was expressive of both the emotional and functional aspects of the building.

The curvilinear forms of Art Noveau are again to be found in the most famous chair of the twentieth century: Mies van der Rohe's cantilever steel Barcelona Chair of 1929. In spite of its functional appearance, the chair was in fact hand made; yet another reminder of Art Nouveau working methods.

The rectilinear mode of Art Nouveau was developed in the twentieth century at the Bauhaus under Walter Gropius and in Holland by the *De Stijl* artists. The geometricity of Mackintosh and Behrens would be stripped down further in the Schroder House (1924), while the Rietveld Chair (1917) would later be transformed into the familiar modern stacking unit furniture. Although rectilinear Art Nouveau is the precursor of the modern style, particularly in architecture, in certain instances architects and designers would revert to the more curving forms. A case in point is Charles Edouard Jeanneret-Gris (1887-1965), more familiarly known as Le Corbusier. Le Corbusier's flat-roofed buidings with their horizontal bands of windows look like Cubist paintings in three dimensions, but in the *Chapel de Notre Dame du Haut* at Ronchamps, Corbusier returned to the more undulating lines of Art Nouveau.

LEFT: *Erich Mendelsohn's influential 1920 Potsdam Tower.*

A Far-Reaching Style

LEFT: De Stijl *artist Gerrit Rietveld designed this* Red Blue Chair *in 1917*.

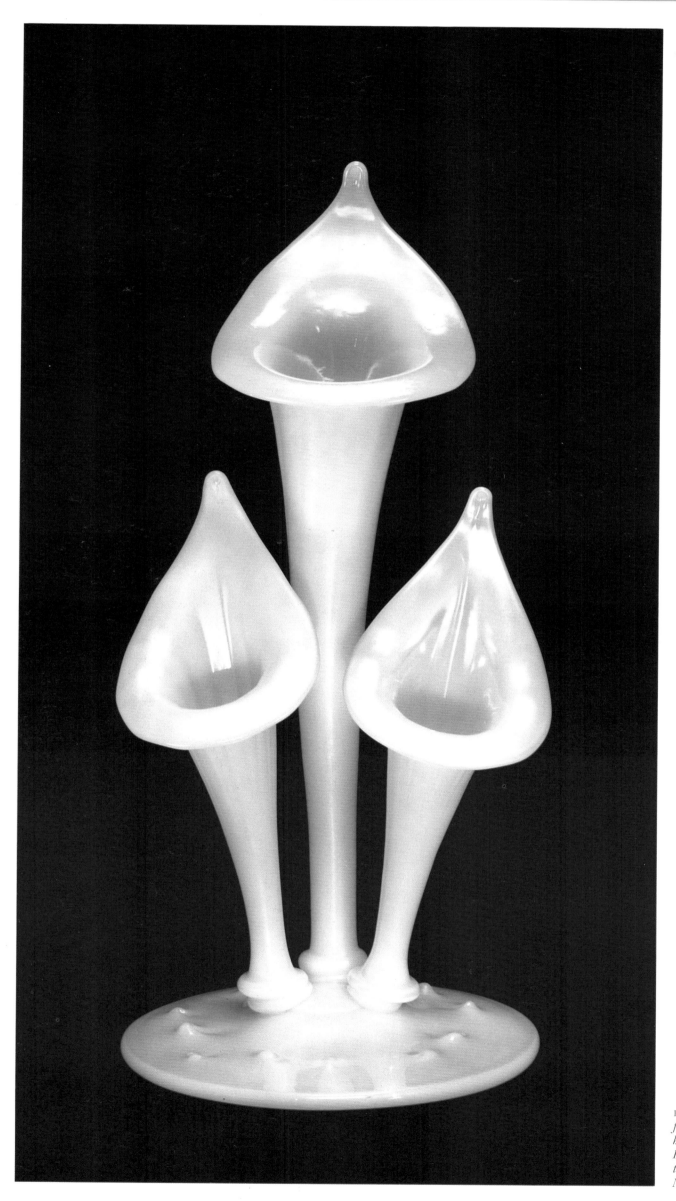

LEFT: *The Art Nouveau love of plant forms persisted well into the 1920s in works such as this lily vase by Frederick Carder of Steuben Glass.*

ABOVE RIGHT: *A 1928 printed textile design by Douglas Cockerel shows the continuing influence of the Arts and Crafts tradition.*

BELOW RIGHT: *This 'Simple Solar' fabric design by Shirley Craven, hand printed on cotton satin by Hull Traders Ltd in 1967, reflects the renewed popularity of Art Nouveau in the 1960s.*

RIGHT: *The Bauhaus Complex at Dessau (1925-26) by Walter Gropius pointed towards the shape of things to come.*

BELOW: *Le Corbusier's church of Notre Dame du Haute at Ronchamps (1950-54) betrays a lingering taste for the curvilinear.*

The importance that had been placed by Art Nouveau designers on plant forms and their structural capabilities, combined with their enthusiasm for new materials, would all be investigated further by modern architects and engineers. Gaudí's parabolic curves would appear again in the reinforced-concrete constructions of Robert Maillart and Hans Levsinger such as the Cement Hall at the Swiss

National Exhibition in Zurich in 1938-9, and the 'leaning tree' system of supports that Gaudí used in the *Sagrada Familia* would be improved upon by Eugène Freyssinet in the underground Basilica of Pius X at Lourdes (1958).

The Art Nouveau pioneers of concrete such as August Perret would extend their influence over many engineers. Felix Candela, a Spanish-born engineer who had fought with the Republicans during the Spanish Civil War, emigrated to Mexico where, for the University City, he designed the Cosmic Ray Lab (circa 1960). Like Gaudí,

Candela made use of a series of hyperbolic parabaloids for the reinforced concrete roof, the strength of the shape allowing him to reduce its thickness to around half an inch. But it is in the TWA Terminal at Kennedy Airport, designed by Eero Saarinen in 1961, that the organic rhythmic forms of the curvilinear tradition of Art Nouveau are most apparent.

As the twentieth century advanced, the belief in the possibility of a purely rational world began to decline and was finally shattered by the events of the World War II. During the following years, there was

LEFT: *Removed from its original setting, this C R Mackintosh table of 1900 appears contemporary.*

RIGHT: *A 1967 metal and marble table by Eero Saarinen echoes the plant forms of Art Nouveau.*

BELOW: *The whiplash curve makes a reappearance on this 1954 MG Model TF.*

a movement away from 'rational'; geometric forms in design; curving, biomorphic forms with a close affinity to those used by the Art Nouveau artists now began to find favor. The functional, straight-lined objects of the 1920s and 1930s were gradually giving way to gentle whiplash curves. Even automobile design felt the influence of this trend as the functionalism of the earlier models gave way to an increased irrationality of form; compare the box-like appearance of an army jeep or a Model T Ford with the curves of a classic British or American car of the 1940s and 1950s. Their design was no longer a mere reflection of their function; the car had become a symbol of prestige, class and power.

With the emergence of Pop Art, artists once again focused as Lautrec had done on everyday urban scenes and domestic objects, and in doing so once again made use of the techniques of poster art. The Art Nouveau posters that celebrated modern life became an important source of approaches and styles. In an effort to achieve harmony with nature and the environment, the pop culture of the 1950s and 1960s promoted a revival of the familiar organic and expressive forms of Art Nouveau. New materials such as plastics, fiberglass and foams facilitated the production of molded chairs with flower-like stems and bases and tulip-shaped seats; thus the new materials facilitated not just a revival, but a genuine extension of Art Nouveau forms.

The psychedelia of the 1960s and early 1970s was perhaps the development that came closest in style to Art Nouveau. Even the drug culture of these years was an aspect shared with many turn-of-the-century Symbolist writers and artists. The pop preoccupation with nostalgia, the desire to 'drop out' of society in favor of a somewhat idealized 'simple life' parallels the Pre-Raphaelites' preoccupation with medieval craft society and the Art Nouveau artists' quest for 'Truth to Nature.' Not surprisingly, therefore, Art Nouveau enjoyed a considerable revival. The original artifacts were prized once more, and imitative designs flourished. Swirling tendrils and Pre-Raphaelite heroines graced shop fronts, record sleeves and rock concert posters. And in the 1960s the symbols of revolution and freedom were those also found in Art Nouveau art and design – the nude and long flowing hair.

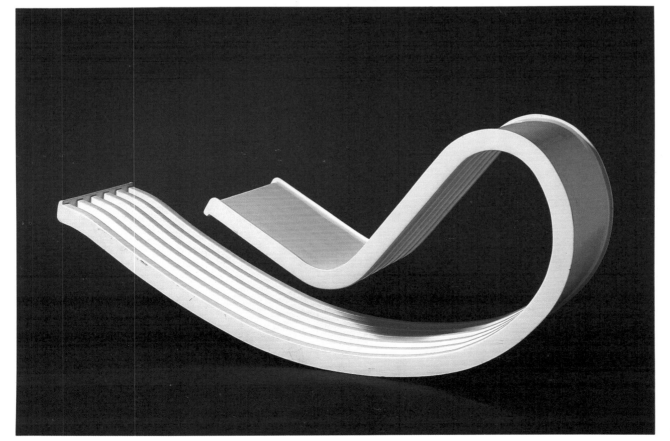

ABOVE LEFT AND RIGHT: *Details of the Guggenheim Museum in New York (1959), by Frank Lloyd Wright. The spiral ramp echoes Gaudí's original plan for the* Casa Mila *in Barcelona.*

LEFT: *'Dondolo' rocking chair in molded fiberglass by Cesare Leonardi and Franca Stragi, first exhibited in Milan in 1968.*

RIGHT: Three figures in a silk dress by Julian Tomchin, *photographed by Hiro (1967).*

Index

Page numbers in *italics* refer to illustrations

Bibliography

Abbate, Francesco (Elizabeth Evans) *Art Nouveau* Octopus, 1972

Amaya, Mario *Art Nouveau* Studio Vista, 1966

Anscombe, Isabelle *A Woman's Touch: Women in Design from 1860 to the Present Day* Virago, 1984

Battersby, Martin *The World of Art Nouveau* Arlington Books, 1968

Bowman, John S *American Furniture* Exeter/Bison Books

Bradbury, Malcolm and McFarlane, James (eds) *Modernism* (Pelican Guide to European Literature) Penguin, 1976

Casanelles, E *Gaudi: A Reappraisal* New York Graphics Society, 1965

Evers H G *The Modern Age* Methuen, 1967

Forty, Adrian *Objects of Desire: Design and Society 1750-1980* Thames and Hudson, 1986

Frampton, Kenneth *Modern Architecture: A Critical History* Thames and Hudson, 1980

Gallo, Max *The Poster in History* New American Library, 1974

Gaunt, William *English Painting* Thames and Hudson

Hanks, David A *The Decorative Designs of Frank Lloyd Wright* Studio Vista, 1979

Hauser, Arnold *The Social History of Art: Vol 4 Naturalism, Impressionism, The Film Age* RKP, 1951

Henderson, Philip *William Morris: His Life, Work and Friends* Thames and Hudson, 1967

Lucie-Smith, Edward *Symbolist Art* Thames and Hudson, 1967

MacCarthy, Fiona *All Things Bright and Beautiful: Design in Britain, 1830 to Today* Allen and Unwin, 1972

Macleod, Robert *C R Mackintosh* Countrylife Books, 1968

Naylor, Gillian *The Arts and Crafts Movement* Studio Vista, 1971

Nuttgens, Patrick *Mackintosh and his Contemporaries* John Murray, 1988

Pevsner, Nikolaus *Pioneers of Modern Design* Penguin, 1960

   The Sources of Modern Architecture and Design Thames and Hudson, 1968

   History of Modern Architecture Vol 1: The Tradition of Modern Architecture MIT Press, 1977

   Studies in Art Architecture and Design: Victorian and After Thames and Hudson, 1968

Pollack, Peter *Picture History of Photography* Abrahams, 1969

Powell, Nicholas *The Sacred Spring* Studio Vista, 1975

Rowland, Kurt *A History of the Modern Movement* Van Rostrand Rheinhold, 1973

Schaefer, Herwin *Nineteenth Century Modern* Praeger, 1970

Sweeney, J J and Sert, J L *Antoni Gaudi* Architectural Press, 1960

Thompson, E P *William Morris: Romantic to Revolutionary* Lawrence and Wishart, 1955

Walken, R A *The Best of Aubrey Beardsley* Chancellor Press, 1985

Watkinson, Roy *William Morris as Designer* Studio Vista, 1967

Acknowledgments

The publisher would like to thank Chris Schüler the editor, Martin Bristow the designer, Moira Dykes the picture researcher and the individuals and agencies listed below for supplying the illustrations:

PICTURE CREDITS

Anderson Collection of Art Nouveau, University of East Anglia, Norwich pages 33 top, center and right, 77 top; T & R Annan and Sons Ltd, Glasgow pages 46, 47, right, 50, 51, 54 below; ARCAID/Richard Bryant pages 44 top, 64 right, 67, 92 both, 93 top; Architectural Association pages 56 right, 64 below, 68, 73 below, 76 top, 38 both; Courtesy of the Art Institute of Chicago/Department of Architecture page 87 center, /Bessie Bennet Fund page 95 top, /Gift of Mr and Mrs Phillip R Dunne page 98 below, /Gift of Malcolm, Kay, Kim and Kyle Kamin page 83, /Gift of Mrs Philip Wrigley page 83 right; The Art Museum, Princeton University page 98 top right; C H Bastin and J Evrard pages 59, 61 top and below, 64 left; Bison Picture Library pages 106 below; The Bridgeman Art Library/Private Collection pages 25 left, 31 below 30 below left; The British Architectural Library, RIBA, London pages 70 both, 73 top left, 75 right, 86 top, 87 below, 102, 103 top; Cassina S P A page 106 top, /The Design Council page 55 below; Martin Charles pages 44 below, 45, 60; Chicago Architectural Society/ Weidenfeld Archive page 86 below; Christie's pages 17 below, 18 both, 19 right, 20, 21 all three, 26 both, 29 top, 31 left, 34 below, 37, 75 left, 84 top, 85, 93 both, 99 both; Conway Library/ Courtauld Institute pages 71, 94 both; The Corning Museum of Glass, Corning, New York pages 22 top and right, 23 right, 24, 25 top and right, 27, 28, 29 below, 104; The Design Council page 17 top; ESTO/Peter Aaron pages 96, 97 both, 98 top left, /Wayne Andrews pages 62, 63, 66 both, 74 top, 87 top, 90 below, 95, /Ezra Stoller page 95 below; Fondation le Corbusier page 103 below; Frank Lloyd Wright Foundation/Weidenfeld Archive page 90 top; Philippe Garner, London/The Bridgeman Art Library page 60; Glasgow School of Art/The Bridgeman Art Library page 49 both; Greater London Photograph Library pages 42 both, 43 both; Angelo Hornak pages 10 top, 22 below left, 23 left, 48, 57 top, 61 center, 69, 72, 73 top left, 96 below, 89, 100; Hunterian Art Gallery, University of Glasgow, Mackintosh Collection pages 47 left, 52 below right, 53, 54 top, 56 left, /The Bridgeman Art Library page 9 below left; Kunstindustrimuseet, Copenhagen pages 8 below, 36 top, Liberty and Co/Weidenfeld Archive pages 11, 12 top, 14, 15 both, 30 top right; Mappin Art Gallery/The Design Council page 30 below; Musée des Arts Decoratifs, Paris/Photo MAD/Sully-Jaumes pages 31 top left, 33 right, 78 top left, 80 below right, /Weidenfeld Archive page 82 both; Musée de l'Ecole de Nancy/Cliche Studio Image Nancy pages 77 below, 81; Museum Bellerive pages 8 top, 33 top; Nordenfjeldske Kunstindustrimuseum, Trondheim pages 9 top, 10 below, 35 top; Österreichische Nationalbibliothek page 74 below; Punch Publications Ltd page 40 below; Royal Pavilion, Art Gallery and Museums, Brighton pages 13 both, 19 left, 35 below, 78 top right and below, 80 top, 84 below; Jessica Strang page 40 top and center; Topham Picture Library page 65; Victoria and Albert Museum, London pages 36 bottom two, 93 left, 105 below, /The Bridgeman Art Library pages 30 top right, 32, 34 top, 52 below left, 105 top; Weidenfeld Archive pages 9 below right, 11, 12 below, 16 both, 55 top, 58 both, 79; Stuart Windsor pages 41 all three, 57 below.